REGION Volume 6, Number 2, 2019

# Cities in the 21<sup>st</sup> century:
# A view from the developing world

Special Issue edited by **David Castells-Quintana** and **Paula Herrera-Idárraga**

## Table of Contents

This special issue on "Cities in the 21$^{st}$ century: A view from the developing world" is edited by David Castells-Quintana (Universidad Autónoma de Barcelona, Barcelona, Spain) and Paula Herrera-Idárraga (Pontificia Universidad Javeriana, Bogotá, Colombia). With the exception of the editorial, all contributions to this special issue have already been published in earlier issues of REGION, for the sake of immediate exposure of the content.

- *An Overview of Urbanization in Ecuador under Functional Urban Area Definition* by Moises Obaco and Juan-Pablo Díaz-Sanchez was originally published in vol. 5, no. 3, 39–48.

- *Agglomeration economies and urban productivity* by Tania Torres-Gutierrez and Jessica Ordoñez was originally published in vol. 6, no. 1, 17–24.

- *Governance of metropolitan areas for delivery of public services in Latin America* by Alejandra Trejo-Nieto, José-Luis Niño-Amezquita and Maria-Luisa Vasquez was originally published in vol. 5, no. 3, 49–73.

- *Market Access and the Concentration of Economic Activity in a System of Declining Cities* by Luis Quintero and Paula Restrepo was originally published in vol. 5, no. 3, 97–109.

**REGION, The journal of ERSA / Powered by WU**
ISSN: 2409-5370, ISBN: 978-3-9504846-3-2

ERSA: http://www.ersa.org
WU: http://www.wu.ac.at

# Editorials

REGION

The Journal of ERSA
Powered by WU

Volume 6, Number 2, 2019, E1–E6
DOI: 10.18335/region.v6i2.260

journal homepage: region.ersa.org

# Cities in the 21$^{st}$ century: A view from the developing world

David Castells-Quintana[1], Paula Herrera-Idárraga[2]

[1] Universidad Autónoma de Barcelona, Barcelona, Spain
[2] Pontificia Universidad Javeriana, Bogotá, Colombia

Received: 12 February 2019/Accepted: 13 February 2019

**Abstract.** In this (introductory) paper, we present i) some basic figures about the rise of cities in the developing world, and ii) the four papers of this special issue. This paper and the other four papers in the issue intend to bring the reality of cities of the developing world in the 21$^{st}$ century to the frontline, hoping to motivate further and much needed research.

**JEL classification:** O1, O4, R1

**Key words:** Cities, urbanisation, developing countries

## 1 Introduction

Internal disparities within countries are sometimes as important, or even more, as international ones. Consequently, our capacity to influence people's welfare depends on our understanding not only of international and national dynamics, but also of what happens between and within regions and cities. Accordingly, research on regional and urban economics has become fundamental for the design of sound policies aimed at increasing prosperity for all.

In recent years and decades, research in the fields of regional and urban economics has gained momentum. This trend follows the reality of a new urban world: the percentage of the world population living in urban areas has increased from around 30 in 1950 to around 54 in 2015, and is expected to reach 66 by 2050 (United Nations 2015). But the focus of research has in most cases been put on the analysis of dynamics of the developed world. By contrast, our understanding of regional and urban dynamics in the developing world remains very limited. Developing countries will by 2030 host more than 85% of the world population, and more than 90% of the new urban residents of the world will live in cities in the developing world (United Nations 2015).

The rise of cities in developing countries becomes evident by looking at some figures. Figure 1 shows urbanisation across different income groups since 1960. In the 1960s, cities in low and lower-middle income countries concentrated between 12 and 20% of their total population, while the figure was 54% in high income countries. Since then, in low and lower-middle income countries urban population has grown by 174% and 125%, respectively. By contrast, in upper-middle and high income countries urban population has grown by 78% and 47%, respectively. Although, in the last two decades the pace

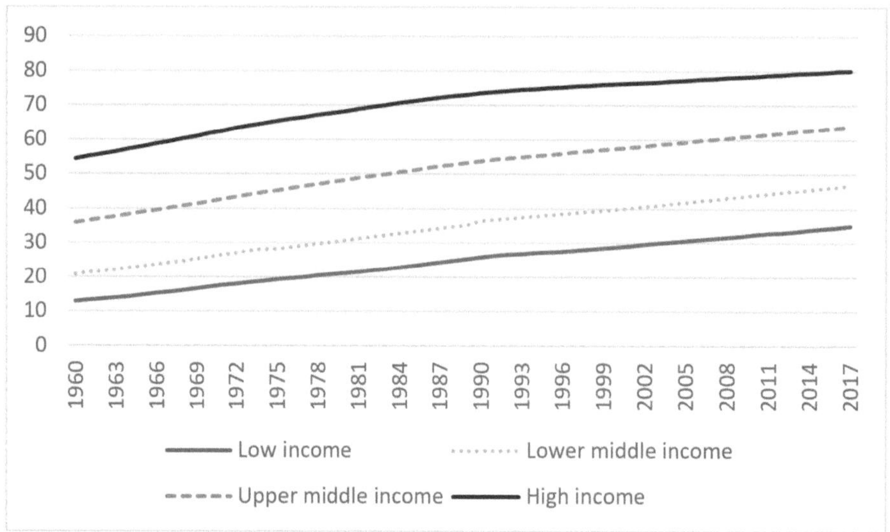


*Source*: World Bank Data

Figure 1: Urban population (% of total)

has decelerated considerably in all countries, the process of urbanisation in developing countries continues to be strong.

This rapid urbanisation worldwide implies an increase in the number as well as in the size of cities. Worldwide, the number of urban agglomerations of more than 300 thousand inhabitants has increased from 304 in 1950 to 1729 in 2015[1]. And the average size of these urban agglomerations has gone from 253 thousand inhabitants in 1950 to 1.268 million in 2015. While in 1950 around 300 million people in the world lived in urban agglomerations of more than 300 thousand inhabitants, this figure exceeds 2.2 billion in 2015, which is almost a third of the total world population, and 57% of the world urban population. And among all urban agglomerations, today the cities of more than 10 million inhabitants concentrate alone more than 12 per cent of the world urban population.

This increase in the number and size of cities has been specially marked in the developing world. In 1975, there were 178 large cities – those with more than one million inhabitants – and 9 megacities – those with more than 10 million inhabitants – in developing countries[2]. In 2015, only a generation after, the number of large cities in developing countries reached 396 (of 494 worldwide), and the number of megacities reached 26 (of 32 worldwide). Twelve of these megacities of the developing world already have more than 20 million inhabitants[3]. In terms of size, 17 out of the top 20 countries with higher average city size are developing countries.

The role of large cities in developing countries is also clear when we look at primate cities (i.e., the largest city in each country). Primate cities in developing countries are, on average, larger than their counterparts in developed countries: in 2010, primate cities in developing countries had on average 3.4 million inhabitants, one million more than their developed counterparts. In developing countries, these cities also concentrate a larger percentage of the urban population. On average, while in developed countries the population in the largest city is nowadays around 35% of the urban population, in the developing world the figure is 43%. For low income countries, as shown in Figure 2, the percentage of urban population living in the largest city is especially high, reaching 56% in 1980. However, since then the figure has decreased, suggesting that new or existing

---

[1]Using World Urbanisation Prospects data (United Nations 2015), and considering urban agglomerations that had at least 300 thousand inhabitants in 1990.

[2]Acknowledging the potential limitations of UN data in what refers to the size of large cities, in these figures we rely on novel data by the Urban Platform of the European Commission. Data refers to "urban areas".

[3]Being Guangzhou, Cairo, Jakarta, Delhi and Calcutta being the 5 largest. In the developed world, only Tokyo has more than 20 million inhabitants.

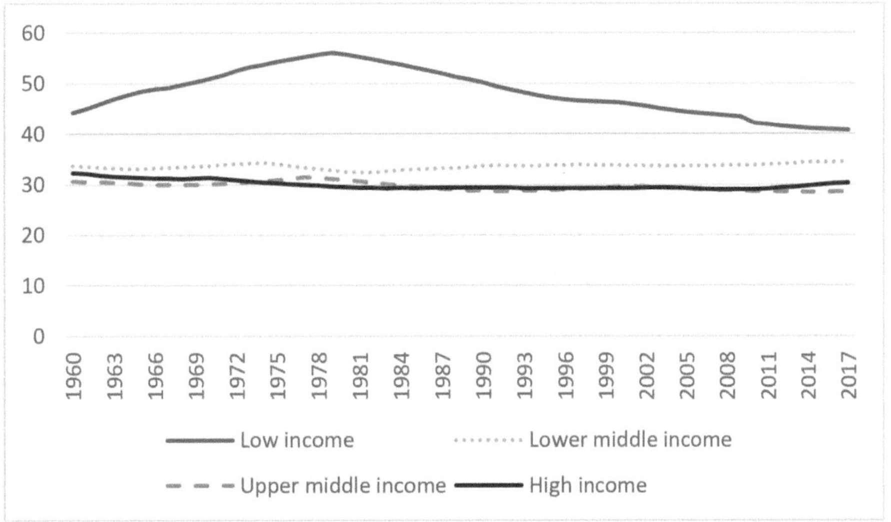


*Source*: World Bank Data

Figure 2: Population in the largest city (% of urban population)

cities beyond the primate city are gaining importance in the last decades in low-income countries.

While this rapid urbanisation and city growth comes with great opportunities, in the form of agglomeration economies (Duranton 2016), it also represents great challenges for sustainable development. Urban residents in developing countries currently face great deficiencies in terms of access to basic services, like access to water, sanitation facilities and electricity (see for instance Graham 2010, Castells-Quintana 2017a,b). As an example, Figure 3 displays the percentage of urban population that has access to electricity. Low income countries still face a huge deficiency in this crucial aspect, which could mean barriers to take advantage of the benefits of urbanisation. Low income countries, and to some extent most developing countries, also face high levels of urban segregation and inequality (Sabatini 2006, López-Morales et al. 2016), and high levels of informality (see for instance Perry et al. 2007, Herrera-Idárraga et al. 2016, García 2017, García, Badillo 2018), among other problems. Our understanding of how these problems evolve, and therefore our capacity to address them, is still very limited.

What becomes evident is that urban patterns have become a key element if we are to understand, and properly address, some of the greatest challenges that developing countries are facing in the 21$^{st}$ century. With this purpose in mind, we have put together this special issue on cities in the 21$^{st}$ century, with a focus on the developing world[4]. In the next section of this introductory paper we present and connect the four papers in the special issue.


## 2   The special issue

The rest of this special issue is composed of four papers. They all study aspects of the reality of developing countries in the 21$^{st}$ century, always from a spatial perspective. Each paper focuses on a different topic, but they nicely complement each other. Likewise, while three papers focus on Latin America and the fourth one on the reality of Eastern Europe and Central Asia, they all have broader implications for the developing world in general. Moreover, by taking a close look at specific cases, these papers provide interesting insights into the developing world, too often missing in the urban and regional economics literature. In this section, we briefly discuss each of these four papers.

---

[4]This special issue was born as an outcome of the PUJ/Banrep: First Workshop in Urban and Regional Economics, held in the Pontificia Universidad Javeriana, in Bogotá in June 2017, where more than 40 papers were presented and discussed.

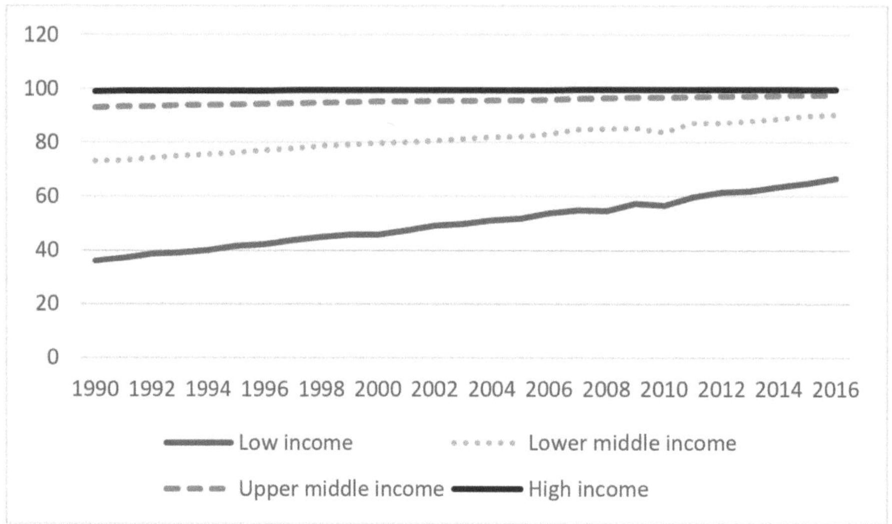



*Source*: World Bank Data

Figure 3: Access to electricity (% of urban population)

**Obaco, M. and Díaz-Sánchez, J. P. (2018) "An Overview of Urbanization in Ecuador under Functional Urban Area Definition", REGION, 5(3), pp. 39-48.**

Defining urban areas, in a consistent and comparable way, is a challenging task. In developing countries, almost by definition, urban areas are changing constantly and rapidly. Understanding how urban areas grow is fundamental for policy makers, for instance in what refers to the planning of infrastructure and the design of sound socio-economic policies. In developed countries, efforts have been put forward to better and more consistently define urban areas. The OECD has defined metropolitan areas using a functional approach based on labour markets and commuting patterns: Functional Urban Areas- FUAs (OECD 2012). In developing countries these efforts have been much more limited. Moises Obaco and Juan-Pablo Díaz-Sanchez (2018) are up to the challenge. They look at urbanisation in Ecuador for more than half a century. Using census data, they reassess the level of urbanisation considering the idea of functional urban areas. They show how urban population in Ecuador today, as probably in many other developing countries, is mainly concentrated in FUA of metropolitan size above 1.5 million inhabitants.

**Torres Gutierrez, T. and Ordóñez, J. (2019) "Agglomeration economies and urban productivity", REGION, 6(1), pp. 17-24.**

In their paper, Tania Torres-Gutierrez and Jessica Ordoñez (2019), also focusing on Ecuador, look at how agglomeration economies have acted to enhance industrial productivity. They do this using census data and studying the evolution of the urban rates and their connection with labour productivity at the municipality level during the last 2 decades of the 20th century and the first one of the 21st. Their study provides evidence on how, under the adequate conditions, urbanisation can be a force for higher productivity in developing countries, as it also has traditionally been in developed countries. However, their results also warn about the risks of congestion in urban areas when urban density becomes too high, something in line with recent papers in the urban economics literature.

**Trejo Nieto, A., Niño Amezquita, J. and Vasquez, M. (2018) "Governance of metropolitan areas for delivery of public services in Latin America", REGION, 5(3), pp. 49-73.**

As shown by the previous two papers, increasing urbanisation in developing countries can lead to larger urban areas, and this brings with it potential benefits in the form of agglomeration economies, but also important challenges and costs. One of the great challenges that large urban areas in developing countries face is the provision of (basic) public services. Alejandra Trejo-Nieto, José-Luis Niño-Amezquita and Maria-Luisa Vasquez (2018), study the provision of public services looking at three major metropolitan areas of Latin America, namely Bogotá, Lima and Mexico City. They analyse how different types of metropolitan governance, in particular jurisdictional fragmentation, influence the performance of these metropolitan areas to provide public services. Their study gives deep insights into how higher fragmentation can represent a challenge for efficient provision of public services. This result is in line, and complements, previous work for OECD metropolitan areas (see for instance Ahrend et al. 2014).

### Quintero, L. and Restrepo, P. (2018) "Market Access and the Concentration of Economic Activity in a System of Declining Cities", REGION, 5(3), pp. 97-109.

Luis Quintero and Paula Restrepo (2018) apparently depart from the other three papers in the issue to study economic activity in declining cities. They study what happens to agglomeration economies in a context of negative population growth. Although most developing countries still face high rates of population growth (mainly in Africa and Asia), other developing countries (for instance in Eastern Europe and Central Asia) are now in later stages of their demographic transition where population growth has gone down substantially. A very interesting result from Quintero and Restrepo's analysis is that in a system of cities facing population loss people will tend to move from small to large cities, increasing concentration in large cities. In this regard, this paper actually connects with the other papers in the issue, where the challenges of increasing urban areas is studied.

---

All in all, this special issue highlights some of the challenges that developing countries face today, and how in the 21$^{st}$ century these challenges are reflected mostly in (large) urban areas. As our understanding of urban dynamics in these areas is still very limited, more research in this regard is urgently needed.

### Acknowledgement

We acknowledge the support of Vicente Royuela in all the process of the special issue, including this introductory paper. We also acknowledge the contribution of all the referees that participated in the issue. Finally, we acknowledge all the participants of the PUJ/Banrep: First Workshop in Urban and Regional Economics, held in the Pontificia Universidad Javeriana, in Bogotá in June 2017. David Castells-Quintana acknowledges the support of ECO2016-75805-R and ECO2016-76855-P.

# References


Ahrend R, Farchy E, Kaplanis I, Lembcke AC (2014) What makes cities more productive? Evidence on the role of urban governance from five OECD countries. OECD-Regional Development Working Papers

Castells-Quintana D (2017a) The city in urban poverty: Book review. *European Journal of Development Research* 29[4]: 942–944. CrossRef.

Castells-Quintana D (2017b) Malthus living in a slum: Urban concentration, infrastructure and economic growth. *Journal of Urban Economics* 98: 158–173. CrossRef.

Duranton G (2016) Agglomeration effects in Colombia. *Journal of Regional Science* 56[2]: 210–238. CrossRef.

García GA (2017) Labor informality: choice or sign of segmentation? A quantile regression approach at the regional level for Colombia. *Review of Development Economics* 21[4]: 985–1017. CrossRef.

García GA, Badillo ER (2018) Rationing of formal sector jobs and informality: The Colombian case. *Journal of International Development* 30[5]: 760–789. CrossRef.

Graham S (2010) *Disrupted Cities: When infrastructure fails.* Routledge, New York. CrossRef.

Herrera-Idárraga P, Lopez-Bazo E, Motellon E (2016) Regional wage gaps, education and informality in an emerging country: The case of Colombia. *Spatial Economic Analysis* 11[4]: 432–456. CrossRef.

López-Morales E, Shin HB, Lees L (2016) Latin American gentrifications. *Urban Geography* 37[8]: 1091–1108. CrossRef.

Obaco M, Díaz-Sánchez JP (2018) Urbanization in Ecuador: An overview using the functional urban area definition. *REGION* 5[3]: 39–48. CrossRef.

OECD (2012) Redefining "urban". OECD Publishing: Paris

Perry G, Maloney W, Arias O, Fajnzyllber P, Mason A, Saavedra-Chanduvi J (2007) Informality and exclusion. The World Bank, Washington DC. CrossRef.

Quintero LE, Restrepo P (2018) Market access and the concentration of economic activity in a system of declining cities. *REGION* 5[3]: 97–109. CrossRef.

Sabatini F (2006) The social spatial segregation in the cities of Latin America. Washington DC, Inter-American Development Bank, Sustainable Development Department

Torres-Gutiérrez T, Ordoñez J (2019) Agglomeration economies and urban productivity. *REGION* 6[1]: 17–24. CrossRef.

Trejo-Nieto A, Niño Amezquita JL, Vasquez ML (2018) Governance of metropolitan areas for delivery of public services: the cases of Bogotá, Lima and Mexico City. *REGION* 5[3]: 49–73. CrossRef.

United Nations (2015) World urbanisation prospects: The 2014 revision. Department of Economic and Social Affairs, Population Division, United Nations, UN DESA Press

# Articles

# REGION

The Journal of ERSA
Powered by WU

Volume 5, Number 3, 2018, 39–48
DOI: 10.18335/region.v5i3.235

journal homepage: region.ersa.org

# Urbanization in Ecuador: An overview using the Functional Urban Area definition

Obaco A. Moisés[1], Díaz-Sánchez Juan Pablo[2]

[1] Universitat de Barcelona, Barcelona, Spain
[2] Escuela Politécnica Nacional, Quito, Ecuador

Received: 28 December 2017/Accepted: 16 October 2018

**Abstract.** This paper presents an overview of the urbanization in Ecuador during the period 1950-2010. First, it is shown that Ecuador does not follow a suitable definition of urban areas, then the idea of Functional Urban Areas (FUAs) definition is introduced. In this line, 28 FUAs in Ecuador are analyzed. When Ecuadorian FUAs population evolution over time is explored, it is possible to observe that the urbanization of Ecuador had its peak between 1960 and 1980. Moreover, the highest increase of population in recent decades is mostly driven by the urban growth of small FUAs. In addition, the analysis suggests that the FUAs in Ecuador are in line with the size and structure of the FUAs of a similar developing country, Colombia, and the whole OECD sample of FUAs. Finally, it is pointed that the population of Ecuador is concentrated in the FUAs of metropolitan size (1.5 million of inhabitants or more), which are below the average of the metropolitan areas of the OECD.

**JEL classification:** R12, R23

**Key words:** Developing economies, Ecuador, FUAs, OECD, Urbanization

## 1 Introduction

Cities are the engines of a country's economic activity. The global urbanization trend over the last decade shows, without doubt, that the world is more urban than rural (Pesaresi et al. 2016). However, how to define "urban" has been an important concern to different international organizations and researchers. In fact, one of the most ambitious goals of the Organization for Economic Co-operation and Development (OECD) and European Commission is to identify and standardize the international comparability of urban areas around the world on the denomination of Functional Urban Areas (FUAs) (OECD 2013, Brezzi et al. 2012).

The FUAs have opened the international comparison of the urbanization to more than 30 OECD and non-OECD countries, and therefore, they allow analysis of the urban spatial structure and its trend across countries under a standardized definition of urban areas (Veneri 2017). The importance of building the FUAs relies on having a new point of view of the urbanization, which becomes important for developing economies because differences in the urbanization between developed and developing economies is remarkable. The urbanization in developing countries is characterized by extreme poverty and low quality institutions (Glaeser, Henderson 2017). Thus, the FUAs have allowed international organizations and governments to consider public policies for better urban planning.

As for the FUAs construction, the FUAs require population and commuting data. However, the lack of necessary data, especially in developing countries, has become a barrier in their identification process. In those cases, several approaches have been used to identify them where there is not standard data available. For example, the OECD applies an alternative method to identify the FUAs in China (OECD 2015). Although, the Chinese FUAs identification does not have the standard methodological approach, they allowed understanding of the urbanization system and economic performance of the Chinese functional urban areas. The result shows that the Chinese FUAs are growing more concentrated with 15 urban areas having more than 10 million inhabitants.

Recently, Obaco et al. (2017) also proposed an alternative approach to identify FUAs. This methodology is applied in Ecuador. However, FUAs identified in Ecuador have not been compared with the international FUAs in the OECD database, differing from was has been done for the majority of other cases. The underlying reason is the fact that Ecuador is not member of the OECD. Thus, this paper contributes analysis of the evolution of urbanization in Ecuador under the FUAs definition and compares the FUAs in Ecuador with the international context of the OECD. Additionally, the contribution of this work to the literature of the FUAs is twofold. First, the comparison of the FUAs of Ecuador in the international context will show whether the Ecuadorian FUAs, based on a different methodological approach, have a similar urban structure of the FUAs of the OECD based on its standard approach. Indeed, comparing FUAs allows further analysis when anomalies in the patterns of countries with similar characteristics are found. Second, this paper will also check the evolution of Ecuadorian urbanization applying a different concept of urbanization.

Results suggest that FUAs in Ecuador are in line with the size and structure of the FUAs of a similar developing country such as Colombia, and the whole OECD sample of FUAs. We also show that the share of the population concentrated in the FUAs of metropolitan size (1.5 million or more) in Ecuador is below the average of urbanization of the OECD sample. When the evolution of the FUAs population is explored, we can observe that the urbanization of Ecuador experienced the highest increase of population between 1960 and 1980. Moreover, another interesting finding is that the highest increase in the population during recent decades is mostly driven by the urban growth of small FUAs.

The rest of this work is structured as follows. Section 2 presents the related literature. Section 3 provides introduction to the urbanization in Ecuador, while section 4 introduces the FUA identification in Ecuador. Section 5 presents the data, while Ecuadorian urbanization through the FUAs definition is presented in section 6. Section 7 shows the Ecuadorian FUAs in the international context. Finally, section 8 presents the conclusions of the paper.


## 2   Related literature

Several approaches have been used to define urban areas. The delimitation of an urban area can be driven by a morphology, demography, or socio-economic point of view (Ferreira et al. 2010). In particular, this work focuses on the economic definition of cities which implies a functional delimitation of urban areas from a socio-economic perspective. In that sense, a city is a dense area that can be considered an independent market in which supply and demand for goods and production factors are traded and an equilibrium price exists.

Commuting flows between cities is, by far, the most popular way to identify a functional city known as Local Labor Market (LLM), which was developed in the US at the beginning of the 90s. Commuting flows are also used for the identification of Metropolitan Areas (Duranton 2015, Puderer 2008, Adams et al. 1999). The use of commuting flows has been widely used in this literature. That is the case of Fox, Kumar (1965) who proposed a method to create local areas based on commuting data, merging spatial areas hierarchically according to workers' daily travels. Similarly, Coombes et al.

(1986), among others, systematized this procedure by developing algorithms that are widely used in many countries and regions in which the idea is to have a minimum of self-containment of commuting flow within the LLMs (Casado-Díaz, Coombes 2011).

However, the international comparability and the collection of statistical data are general problems as most countries use different conceptions to define their metropolitan areas. One of the most ambitious efforts of the Organization for Economic Cooperation and Development (OECD), jointly with the European Commission, is the identification and standardization of the economic urban areas labelled as Functional Urban Areas (FUAs). This methodology identifies 1,251 FUAs of different sizes in more than 31 countries, which produced the OECD metropolitan dataset, which considers close to 300 cities with populations of 500,000 inhabitants or more. Currently, many researchers prefer the use of FUAs to perform economic analyses (OECD 2013, 2016, Schmidheiny, Suedekum 2015, Veneri 2016, 2017) instead of simply geographical delimitations.[1] For example, Veneri (2016) finds a better fitting model for the zip's law using FUAs rather than the administrative boundaries given by the countries, and Veneri (2017) analyzes the urban spatial structure of the FUAs across the world and find that there is an increasing trend in the decentralization of the urban areas. Moreover, Ahrend et al. (2017) and Matano et al. (2018) analyze agglomeration effects on labor productivity using FUAs as units of analysis.

In detail, FUAs involve three identification steps (OECD 2013). First, it explores the population density of the country, looking for grid cells of high population density (grid cells with a minimum of 1,000 or 1,500 inhabitants – set by the researcher – per km2). Next, it identifies clusters of grid cells of high population density. Those clusters should contain a minimum of 50,000 or 100,000 inhabitants to be considered an urban core, depending on the country. These urban cores allow the identification of the municipality of reference (head of the FUAs). However, a minimum of 50% of the population must be contained in the urban core. In the second step, those urban centers are connected as part of one FUA if two urban cores share at least a minimum commuting flow (15%).[2] In a third step, the hinterland is identified, which includes all the surrounded areas that are not urban areas but connected to the urban cores through a minimum commuting flow as well. The minimum is the same that has been applied in the second step.

The OECD concept of FUAs has also been extended to those countries that are not OECD members because generally they do not account for their own economic definition of urban areas. In this case, the FUAs allow to compare, to evaluate, and to elaborate recommendations of public policies and urbanization around the world. However, the lack of adequate data to elaborate the FUAs is a main barrier in these countries. For example, in China (OECD 2015), the very same OECD modifies the FUAs methodology to take advantage of the available information or characteristics of the country. In this case, a different minimum threshold to identify urban cores is applied (550 inhabitants per km2) as this country is not densely populated across the territory. To connect urban cores and determine the hinterland, it is applied a decay function of the expected commuting zone.

Similarly, Obaco et al. (2017) present a different methodology to identify FUAs where there is not commuting data. The approach is based on a varying travel time to connect urban cores and determine the hinterland of each FUA. The final coverage of the travel time will depend on the geographical extension of the urban cores because it is shown that larger urban cores have on average more influence zones. However, this model needs a calibration of the parameters to apply the varying travel time model. The model is based on the estimated parameters from Colombia (For more detail, see Obaco et al. 2017). Then, the model is applied in Ecuador. Following this work, and the simplicity of the model to identify FUAs, the OECD has used the same travel time approach to identify FUAs in other developing countries such as Morocco and Viet Nam (OECD 2018). However, the FUAs identified in Ecuador have not been explored and have not been compared with the international OECD database. In this work, we cover this gap.

---

[1]For more information and list of countries, see http://www.oecd.org/cfe/regional-policy/functional-urbanareasbycountry.htm

[2]Polycentric FUAs is where there are two or more urban cores within the FUA. In many European countries the minimum commuting flows applied might reach up to 50% (OECD 2012).

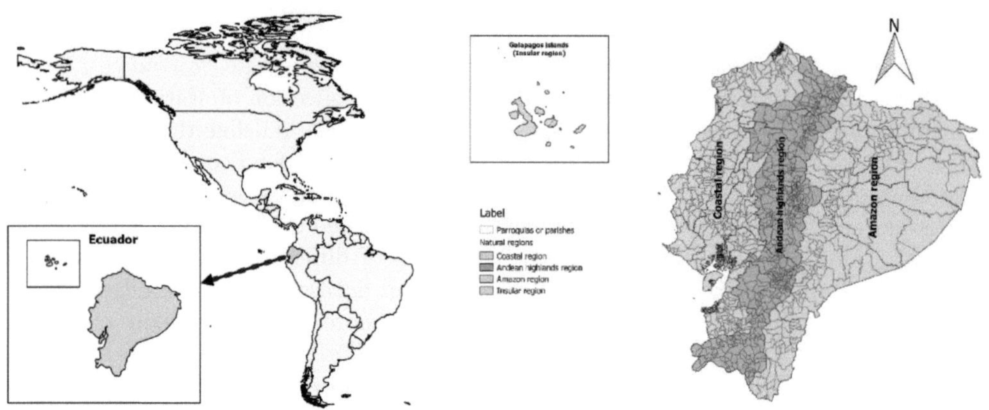



*Source*: INEC-Ecuador, Administrative boundaries based on the year 2010
*Notes*: Elaboration by the authors

Figure 1: Ecuador

## 3  Urban definition in Ecuador

Ecuador is a small developing open economy. It lies on northwest coast of South America. It limits with Colombia at the north, Peru at the east and south, and the Pacific Ocean at the west (see panel A of Figure 1). Ecuador has an area of 283,561 km2 and it is formed by four natural regions: The Coast, the Highlands, the Amazon and the Galapagos Islands. Administrative division of Ecuador is based on three levels. From higher to lower: provinces (25), cantons (224), and parishes (1,024), (see panel B of Figure 1)[3]. Provinces are the most aggregated administrative division; meanwhile parishes are the closest to the conceptualization of municipality. Ecuadorian authorities consider urban areas as inhabitants living in the head of each canton, otherwise they are rural areas. Thus, this characterization of urban does not consider peripheral population beyond the head of the cantons.

In terms of population, Ecuador has about 17 million inhabitants in 2018. In terms of ethnicity composition, Ecuador has a variety of self-identification ethnic groups such as mestizo (majoritarian), indigenous, white, black, and others. As for the urbanization, it is considered that Ecuador has faced a rapid urbanization process since 1960 (Villacis, Carrillo 2012). The current urbanization rate is about 65%, being lower than the average of Latin America around 70%. However, Ecuadorian urbanization process is characterized by extreme poverty. It is estimated that around 35% of the urban population in Ecuador lived in slums in 2014 (UN 2015).

Considering the Ecuadorian authority definition of urban as a starting point, most of the population is concentrated in two urban parishes: Guayaquil, which is in the Coast, and Quito, which is in the Highlands. According to the 2010 census, these two cities have 27% of the total population, and the 35% of the total urban population; thus, these two urban areas could be considered as metropolitan cities, however only Quito has this category[4].

## 4  FUAs identification in Ecuador

As it was mentioned, the urban identification in Ecuador does not follow international standards of urban areas. Thus, we cannot determine the total number of cities existing in Ecuador. We focus only in the FUAs identification to explore urbanization in Ecuador.

We use the FUAs identification made by Obaco et al. (2017)[5]. These authors used

---

[3]Numbers of administrative divisions according to the 2010 census of population and dwelling.

[4]According to the 2010 census, the four most populated cities are Guayaquil has 2,291,158 inhabitants, Quito has 1,619,146, Cuenca has 331,888 and Santo Domingo has 305,632 inhabitants.

[5]For further detail, see Obaco et al. (2017).

satellite imagery of LandScan data to identify population density and travel time using the road network system of Google maps and Open Street Maps to cover the connection between urban cores and the hinterlands. Data used for the identification is between 2010 and 2014. The novelty of this approach is provided by allowing varying of the travel time according to the parameters of expansion that are calculated on the geographical extension of the urban cores. The parameters for the travel time model are based on the commuting flows of Colombia. Then, it is applied in Ecuador. The preferred identification of FUAs is determined by which allows to verification of more urban cores across the country. As Ecuador is not a densely populated country, authors analyze the 28 FUAs that were identified under a minimum threshold of 500 inhabitants or more per squared kilometer and 25,000 inhabitants in order to be considered as an urban core. The 28 FUAs allow to have representative urban cores in the Amazon (not highly populated region). They are composed by 34 urban cores in Ecuador, allowing for some polycentricity structure. If the thresholds were increased to the minimum applied by the OECD (1,000 inhab. and 50,000 inhab. to be an urban core), 20 urban cores could be identified with a total of 20 FUAs. Thus, we present the main analysis using the 28 FUAs. Moreover, results do not change when the 20 FUAs are analyzed as they are mostly small sized. Thus, the model was validated on sensibility test and robustness checks.

Figure 2 shows the 28 identified FUAs in Ecuador. The Ecuadorian FUAs system is majorly dominated by small FUAs. The two FUAs of metropolitan size are Guayaquil and Quito. There are 11 FUAs in the Coastal region, 13 in the Highlands, and 4 in the Amazon. Thus, we have a sample that covers urbanization even in the less populated zones of Ecuador. In Galapagos, the population density is much lower than in the Amazon, thus the Galapagos Islands are not included in the final list of FUAs. The Ecuadorian FUAs show the heterogeneous composition in terms of administrative boundaries because they are very small in the Highland, and large in Coastal and Amazon regions. However, the administrative boundaries are relatively large compared with the urban core extension in most of the cases. The FUAs cover around 7% of the total country extension and the two metropolitan areas around 3% of the total country's extension.

## 5   Data

We use information from the Ecuadorian censuses in order to explore the urbanization process over time. The first census was in 1950. The historical population comes from the National Institute of Statistical and Census (INEC)[6]. To compare the FUAs of Ecuador with the international OECD dataset, we divide the OECD's FUA in four groups: OECD, Europe, Colombia and Ecuador.

## 6   Urbanization in Ecuador

Figure 3 shows the total FUAs population according to their respective Ecuadorian censuses. The number of people living in FUAs has rapidly increased between 1950 and 2010. In 1950, the total FUAs population was around 40% of the total population, being mostly settled in the rural area. In 1972, the population living in FUAs reached around 50% of the total; and, in 1990, the population living in FUAs reached 60%. For 2010, the total population living in FUAs is around 63%. Thus, the highest increase in the urban population is presented from 1962 to 1982, around 0.77% per year.

Table 1 shows the average of the FUAs size distribution of the 28 FUAs according to the information gathered in the censuses. In 1950, the FUAs size distribution was below 0.5 million, composed of 26 FUAs below 0.2 million and 2 FUAs between 0.2 and 0.5 million. In 1990, the first FUAs of large metropolitan size appear, with one FUA between 0.5 and 1.5 million, 3 FUAs between 0.2 and 0.5 million, and 23 FUAs below 0.2 million. In 2010, the distribution was: 2 FUAs larger than 1.5 million, no FUAs between 0.5 and

---

[6]The data from Ecuador is available at http://www.ecuadorencifras.gob.ec/banco-de-informacion/. Moreover, we assume that the geographical extension of the FUAs identified through the period 2014-2010 are the same and fixed over time, because there is not information of the historical boundaries of the parishes over the time. The OECD database is available at http://www.oecd.org/cfe/regional-policy/-functionalurbanareasbycountry.htm.

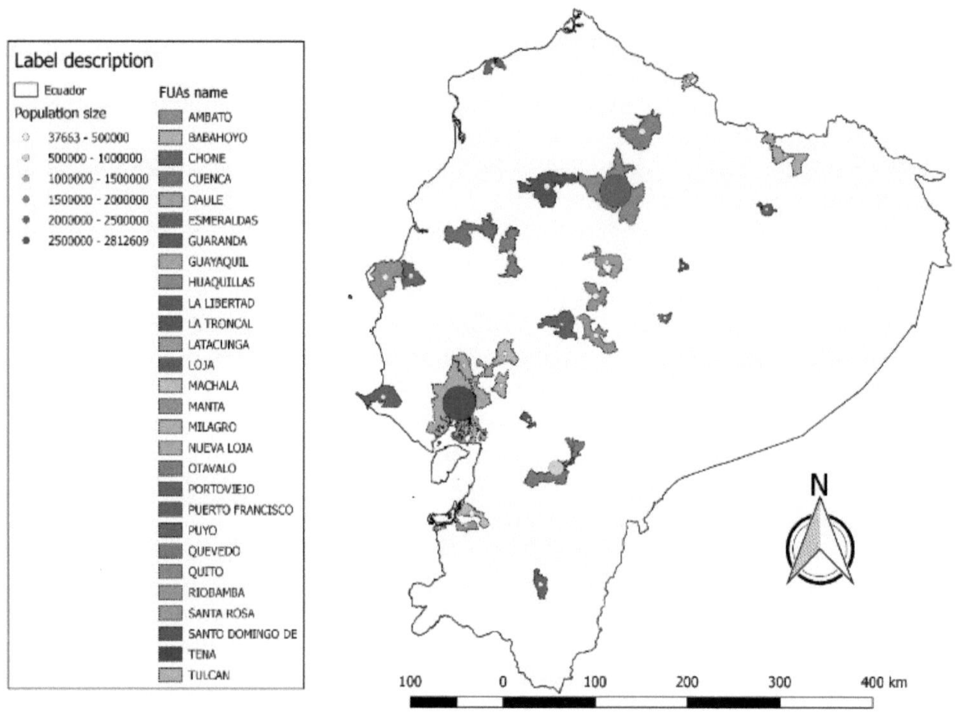


*Source*: INEC-Ecuador, and Obaco et al. (2017). Administrative boundaries and population based on the year 2010-2014
*Notes*: Elaboration by the authors

Figure 2: FUAs in Ecuador

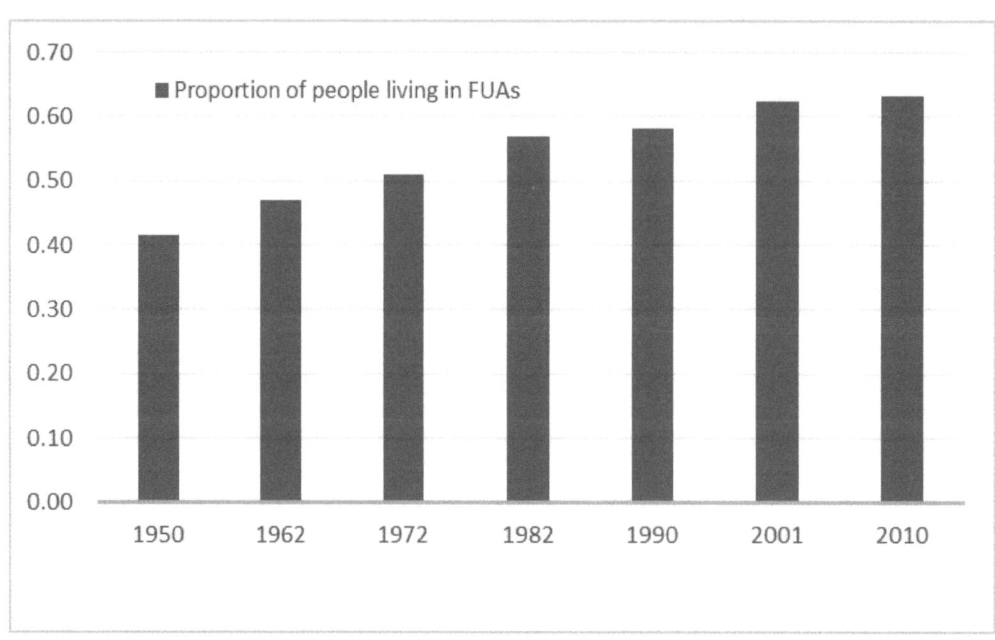


*Source*: INEC, Ecuador
*Notes*: Elaboration by the authors

Figure 3: Population living in the FUAs

Table 1: FUAs size distribution in Ecuador (Average size)

| FUAs | 1950 | 1962 | 1974 | 1982 |
|---|---|---|---|---|
| FUAs greater than 1.5 M | | | | |
| FUAs between 0.5 and 1.5 M | | 544,506 | 812,374 | 1,173,644 |
| FUAs between 0.2 and 0.5 M | 292,986 | 458,255 | | 253,454 |
| FUAs less than 0.2 M | 28,577 | 42,476 | 65,218 | 79,505 |
| no FUAs | 1,873,765 | 2,368,872 | 3,201,281 | 3,472,337 |
| Total Population | 3,202,757 | 4,476,007 | 6,521,710 | 8,060,712 |

| FUAs | 1990 | 2001 | 2010 |
|---|---|---|---|
| FUAs greater than 1.5 M | 1,611,884 | 2,028,966 | 2,436,027 |
| FUAs between 0.5 and 1.5 M | 1,376,630 | | |
| FUAs between 0.2 and 0.5 M | 245,632 | 284,534 | 291,813 |
| FUAs less than 0.2 M | 80,529 | 91,241 | 86,048 |
| no FUAs | 4,070,608 | 4,566,649 | 5,316,535 |
| Total Population | 9,648,189 | 12,156,608 | 14,483,499 |

*Source*: INEC, Ecuador
*Notes*: Elaboration by the authors

1.5 million, 10 FUAs between 0.2 and 0.5 million, and the remaining (16 FUAs) were below 0.2 million.

Figure 4 presents the average of the urban primacy of the FUAs in Ecuador for the period 1950-2010. We can observe the primacy of the two largest FUAs, Guayaquil and Quito during the whole period of time. However, in the most recent decades, the urban population has been mainly driven by the small FUAs, while the largest cities have grown slowly. For example, from 1962-1982, the largest urban population change was experienced in the Amazon and Coastal cities.

## 7 The international context

Figure 5 shows the composition of the Ecuadorian FUAs system and a comparison to OECD countries, Europe, and Colombia in the year 2014. The comparison to Colombia is relatively important because Ecuador and Colombia share borders[7]. 53 FUAs were identified in Colombia. As we can see, both systems are quite homogeneous. The Ecuadorian urban structure is still growing, and this growth is based on the small and medium sized FUAs (lower than half million inhabitants). If we compare the FUAs in Ecuador identified with the minimum threshold applied by the OECD, the same structure of these FUAs is based on the small FUA size. Additionally, a weak composition of metropolitan size (between 0.5 and 1.5 million inhabitants) is observed.

Clearly, Ecuadorian FUAs structure follows the international pattern. Europe is the exception since it has a more diverse composition. Furthermore, like Ecuador, Colombia has larger administrative boundaries compared with the real extensions of the urban cores.

Figure 6 shows the share of population contained in the FUAs of metropolitan size with respect to the total population by country. When the FUAs of metropolitan size (Guayaquil and Quito) in Ecuador are compared with 290 FUAs of metropolitan size of 32 countries, the Ecuadorian metropolitan areas are below the global average, and even below their Latin America partners (Colombia, Chile, and Mexico)[8]. The same results are obtained when we compared with the 20 FUAs of different threshold.

---

[7]The Latin America sample of FUAs considers Mexico, Chile, and Colombia. We use this year because the FUAs of Ecuador and Colombia have full information for this year. The OECD sample does not present information either for the FUAs of Ecuador and Colombia.

[8]Information of the FUAs was gathered from https://measuringurban.oecd.org/#story=0, the Information of Ecuador was taken from Obaco et al. (2017). Information about Turkey and China are not

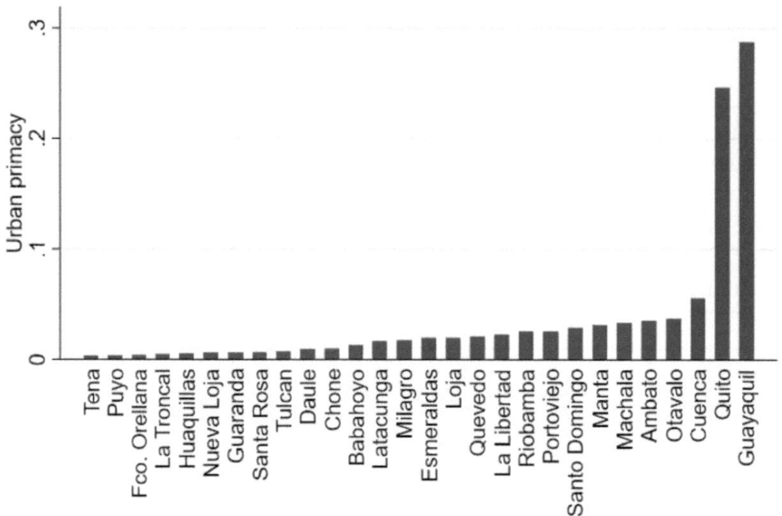



*Source*: INEC, Ecuador
*Notes*: Elaboration by the authors

Figure 4: Ecuadorian Urban Primacy Structure (average of all censuses)

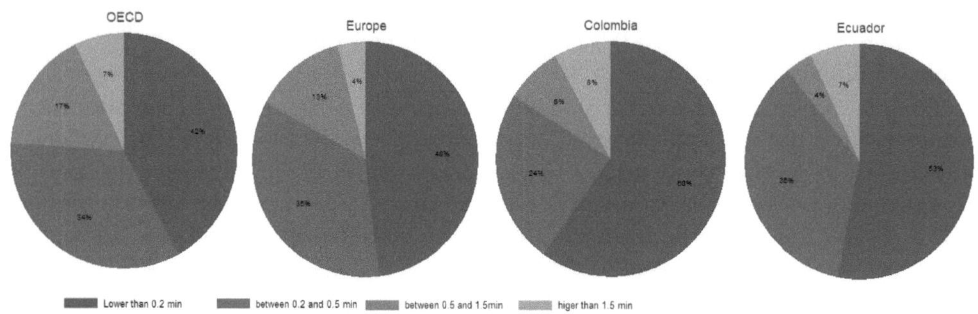



*Source*: Information taken from OECD and INEC, Ecuador
*Notes*: Elaboration by the authors

Figure 5: FUAs size classification in the year 2014

## 8    Conclusions

This work presents the urbanization process of Ecuador using the concept of Functional Urban Area and also compares with the international context. As for the urbanization in Ecuador, we part for two main considerations. First, the Ecuadorian official definition of urban, which is basically the population living in the head of the canton, does not approach an international conceptualization of urban areas nor FUAs. Second, the lack of commuting data does not allow application of any standard functional delimitation of urban areas in this country. These two important facts are limitations for and adequate planning of urban areas.

Later, we analyze 28 FUAs identified in Ecuador. Most FUAs are small size, one of medium size, and two of large metropolitan sizes in Ecuador. The largest increase of the urban population was during the period of 1962-1982. Additionally, the two largest cities, Guayaquil and Quito, remain larger over time, although the urban growth is mainly driven by the small FUAs in the last decades. This is important because it could show some trend to the decentralization of the urban system.

Next, we compare the data of Ecuador with the international database of the OECD. The FUAs of Ecuador also follow the composition of the urban structure of Colombia

available yet.

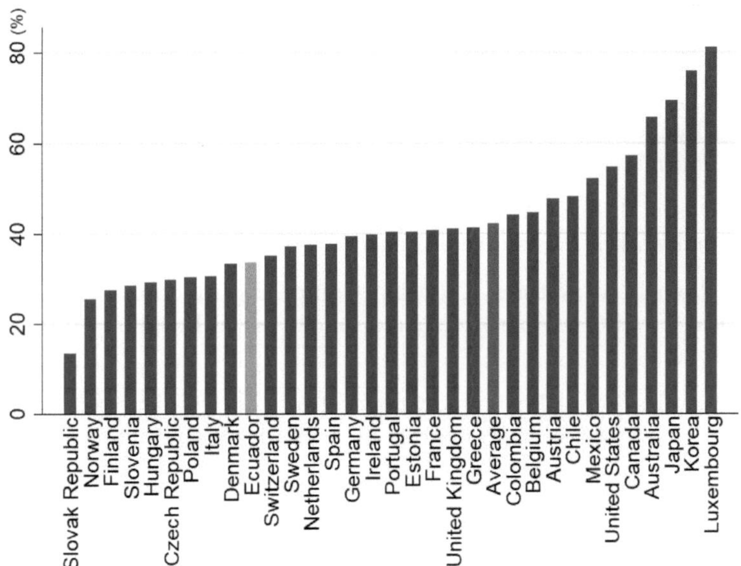


*Source*: Information taken from OECD and INEC, Ecuador
*Notes*: Elaboration by the authors

Figure 6: Share of metropolitan areas in overall population in the year 2014

and the whole sample of the OECD composed mainly of small FUAs size. Moreover, the largest two Ecuadorian cities are below the average of the metropolitan FUAs of the OECD.

Finally, we highlight the importance of standardizing the concept of urban areas to give a better comparison among countries. In this line, the OECD presents an important advance in the collection of data shown in this work.

## References

Adams JS, VanDrasek BJ, Phillips EG (1999) Metropolitan area definition in the United States. *Urban Geography* 20[8]: 695–726. CrossRef.

Ahrend R, Farchy E, Kaplanis I, Lembcke A (2017) What makes cities more productive? Evidence from five OECD countries on the role of urban governance. *Journal of Regional Science* 57[3]: 385–410. CrossRef.

Brezzi M, Piacentini M, Sanchez-Serra D (2012) Measuring metropolitan areas: A comparative approach in OECD countries. In: Fernández Bazquez E, Rubiera Morellón F (eds), *Defining the Spatial Scale in Modern Regional Analysis: New Challenges from Data at Local Level*. Advances in Spatial Science, Springer, 71-89. CrossRef.

Casado-Díaz JM, Coombes M (2011) The delineation of 21st century local labour market areas: A critical review and a research agenda. *Boletín de la Asociación de Geógrafos Españoles* 57: 7–32

Coombes MG, Green AE, Openshaw S (1986) An efficient algorithm to generate official statistical reporting areas: The case of the 1984 travel-to-work areas revision in Britain. *Journal of the Operational Research Society* 37: 943–953. CrossRef.

Duranton G (2015) A proposal to delineate metropolitan areas in Colombia. *Desarrollo y Sociedad* 75: 223–264. CrossRef.

Ferreira JA, Condessa B, Castro e Almeida J, Pinto P (2010) Urban settlements delimitation in low-density areas. An application to the municipality of Tomar (Portugal). *Landscape and Urban Planning* 97[3]. CrossRef.

Fox KA, Kumar TK (1965) The functional economic area: Delineation and implications for economic analysis and policy. *Papers and Proceedings of the Regional Science Association* 15: 57–85. CrossRef.

Glaeser EL, Henderson JV (2017) Urban economics for the developing world: An introduction. *Journal of Urban Economics* 98[1]: 1–5. CrossRef.

Matano A, Obaco M, Royuela V (2018) What drives the spatial wage premium for formal and informal workers? The case of Ecuador. AQR-IREA working paper (6): 35

Obaco M, Royuela V, Vítores X (2017) Computing functional urban areas using a hierarchical travel time approach: An applied case in Ecuador. AQR-IREA working paper (5): 46

OECD – Organization of Economic Cooperation and Development (2012) Redefining urban: A new way to measure metropolitan areas. OECD Publishing, Paris

OECD – Organization of Economic Cooperation and Development (2013) Definition of functional urban areas (FUA) for the OECD metropolitan database. OECD Publishing, Paris

OECD – Organization of Economic Cooperation and Development (2015) OECD urban policy reviews: China. OECD Publishing, Paris

OECD – Organization of Economic Cooperation and Development (2016) Making cities work for all. Data and actions for inclusive growth. OECD Publishing, Paris

OECD – Organization of Economic Cooperation and Development (2018) OECD urban policy reviews: VietNam. OECD Publishing, Paris

Pesaresi M, Melchiorri M, Siragusa A, Kemper T (2016) Atlas of the human planet 2016: Mapping human presence on earth, with the global human settlement layer. European Commission, EUR – Scientific and Technical Research Reports

Puderer H (2008) Defining and measuring metropolitan areas: A comparison between Canada and the United States geography. Geography working paper series defining, 92, 1-12

Schmidheiny K, Suedekum J (2015) The pan-European population distribution across consistently defined functional urban areas. *Economics Letters* 133: 10–13. CrossRef.

UN – United Nations (2015) World urbanization prospects: The 2014 revision. Department of Economic and Social Affairs, Population Division, (ST/ESA/SER.A/366)

Veneri P (2016) City size distribution across the OECD: Does the definition of cities matter? *Computers, Environment and Urban Systems* 59: 86–94. CrossRef.

Veneri P (2017) Urban spatial structure in OECD cities: Is urban population decentralising or clustering? *Papers in Regional Science*. CrossRef.

Villacis B, Carrillo D (2012) Estadística Demográfica en el Ecuador: Diagnóstico y Propuestas. Instituto Nacional de Estadística y Censos (INEC) Quito, Ecuador

The Journal of ERSA
Powered by WU

REGION

Volume 6, Number 1, 2019, 17–24
DOI: 10.18335/region.v5i3.242

journal homepage: region.ersa.org

# Agglomeration economies and urban productivity

**Tania Torres-Gutiérrez[1], Jessica Ordóñez[1]**

[1] Universidad Técnica Particular de Loja, Loja, Ecuador

Received: 26 January 2018/Accepted: 21 November 2018

**Abstract.** This study explores the relationship between agglomeration economies and industrial productivity between 1980 and 2010 in Ecuador. The measure of productivity used is labor productivity. We conclude that urbanization economies have a positive impact on productivity in the period analyzed. These results are consistent with other works for developed and developing countries.

**JEL classification:** R12

**Key words:** agglomeration, agglomeration economies, urban productivity, Ecuador

## 1    Introduction

The increasing concentration of people and production produces benefits known as economies of agglomeration in the economic literature. Traditionally, agglomeration economies are classified in location economies and urbanization economies.

From the seminal works of Glaeser et al. (1992) and Henderson et al. (1995), the ongoing debate is not only about the dichotomy between specialized and diversified environments within the same urban system, but also about the coexistence of specialization and diversity.

Following Glaeser et al. (1992), location economies or MAR[1] externalities that operate within a specific industry restrict the flow of ideas to others, allowing the innovator to internalize externalities. Such interactions can positively influence the productivity of companies and the growth of cities. On the other hand, the urbanization of economies occurs through industries, which motivates the argument of Jacobs (1969) that the variety of industries within a geographical region promotes knowledge spillovers and results in innovative activities and economic growth. In this framework, the concepts of specialization and diversification are inherent to the economies of location and urbanization, respectively.

The empirical literature establishes that spatial concentration of industrial activity improves economic growth, productivity, and innovation through different approaches, among which the common denominator is the analysis of the location-urbanization dichotomy. In line with this literature, this study explores the relationship between the economies of agglomeration and industrial productivity between 1980 and 2010, years for which census data exist for the economic activity of the country. There are two motivations for this work. First, to contrast the economic literature and the empirical results broadly focused in developed countries with those of a developing country like

---

[1]Refers to the model presented by Marshall (1890), Arrow (1962), and Romer (1986).

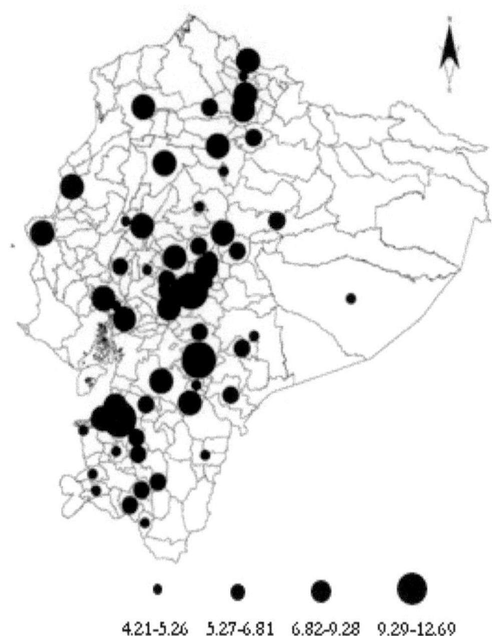


*Source*: Own elaboration based on INEC data

Figure 1: Average annual growth of productivity in the cantons of Ecuador: 1980 – 2010

Ecuador. Second, to contribute to the orientation and reform of economic policies related to the productivity of the country, which seeks to reorient its strong agro-export sector.

## 2   Industrial dynamism: Diversity of the cantons of Ecuador

The industrial sector is the second most important in terms of GDP in the Ecuadorian economy, but it is the most dynamic given that, unlike the other sectors, it has experienced 9% growth between 1980 and 2010 according to World Bank data. The services sector is the most relevant due to, among other things, the momentum generated in the eighties by exports and the oil boom that stimulated this sector, as well as that of the public administration. This is compounded by the significant growth in self-employed activities in the tertiary sector, whose participation in the national economically active population (EAP) in 1974 was 8.4%, 11.1% in 1982, and 28.5% in 2010. Finally, agriculture has fallen in its share of the national GDP by 6% in this period.

As in other countries, economic activity tends to agglomerate in relatively few cities: Guayaquil and Quito mainly, those that from colonization maintain their supremacy over the others, and therefore perform important economic, regional, and international functions. Although these cities have altogether only 3.29% of the total surface area, they contain 16.25% and 15.48% of the population, they generate 23.61% and 25.19% of the gross added value, and represent 21.35% and 28.91% of manufacturing employment, respectively. Based on the information available for Ecuador at the industry and canton level, Figure 1 shows the productivity growth in the analysis period for cantons whose increase is above the average annual growth rate of 4.2%.

## 3   Data and variables

To determine if agglomeration economies affect productivity, we used data from the 1980 and 2010 Economic Census of the National Institute of Statistics and Censuses (INEC), at the level of each sector and canton or municipality, except for those corresponding to the Galapagos Islands. The empirical work included the homogenization of the databases prepared from the referred censuses because these were not directly comparable. In total,

Table 1: Summary statistics of the main variables

| Variable | Mean | Standard Deviation |
|---|---|---|
| productivity growth | .127 | 1.391 |
| specialization | -.097 | .815 |
| diversity | -.983 | .470 |
| density | -1.711 | 1.958 |
| average size firms | -.2509 | .609 |

*Notes*: The productivity growth is between 1980 and 2010. All variables refer to logarithms

26 sectors and 114 cantons are integrated. The sectoral breakdown corresponds to two digits and three digits - ISIC for 1980 and 2010, respectively.

The dependent variable is measured as follows:

$$\Delta prod_{ic} = \frac{\log(Y_{ic-2010}/emp_{ic-2010})/(Y_{i-2010}/emp_{i-2010})}{\log(Y_{ic-1980}/emp_{ic-1980})/(Y_{i-1980}/emp_{i-1980})} \tag{1}$$

where, $Y_{ic}$ and $emp_{ic}$ are the levels of production and employment by industry and canton, respectively, between 1980 and 2010.

### 3.1 Measuring agglomeration economies

The measure of agglomeration economies is the index of specialization related to location economies:

$$esp_{ic} = \frac{emp_{ic}/emp_c}{emp_i/emp} \tag{2}$$

where, $emp_{ic}$ is the employment of industry $i$ in canton $c$, and $emp$ is total employment.

While the economies of urbanization are commonly measured through the inverse of the Herfindahl index, constructed from the participation of industries in local employment, with the exception of the industry that is considered, this variable is normalized by the same variable at the country level:

$$div_{ic} = \frac{1/\sum_{i*=1,i*\neq i}^{i}[emp_{i*c}/(emp_c - emp_{ic})]^2}{1/\sum_{i*=1,i*\neq i}^{i}[emp_{i*}/(emp - emp_i)]^2} \tag{3}$$

where $i$ is the number of industries. The numerator is maximum when all sectors, except the subject of the analysis, $i*$, are the same size in the cities. This indicator reflects the sectorial diversity of the industry and the city. Therefore, it is not necessarily related to the level of specialization of the industry being analyzed.

With the intuition that large companies are usually better able than small companies to internalize some of the local effects, Glaeser et al. (1992) suggest incorporating the average size of firms within the local industry as an additional determinant of location economies. When normalized by the average of the companies in the industry at the level of the whole country, we obtain:

$$size_{ic} = \frac{emp_{ic}/n_{ic}}{emp_i/n_i} \tag{4}$$

where $n_{ic}$ is the number of companies in the industry and in city $c$. However, according to Combes, Gobillon (2015), its use leads to serious problems of endogeneity, since it depends on the location options of the companies and their scale of production, which directly influence local productivity. Thus, one should avoid introducing it into the specification unless you have a strong instrumentation strategy.

Finally, as in Combes (2000), to simultaneously control for differences between cities, it is relevant to consider the density of total employment by means of the following indicator:

$$den_c = \frac{emp_c}{area_c} \tag{5}$$

where $area_c$ is the area of the city measured in km$^2$.

### 3.2 Selection bias

A particularity of the data used in this study is that they are not fully observable, since some industrial sectors are present only in certain cities. This is a typical problem in research that uses data on a local scale. We isolate the selection bias through a model Heckman (1979) proposes, applied in two stages as in Viladecans-Marsal (2004), Combes (2000), Henderson et al. (1995), and others. In the first stage, a model is formulated to estimate the probability that a city contains an industrial sector:

$$Prob(S = 1|Z) = \Phi(Z\gamma) \tag{6}$$

where $S$ indicates the sector ($S = 1$ if the sector is in the city and $S = 0$ otherwise), $Z$ is a vector of explanatory variables, $\gamma$ is a vector of unknown parameters, and $\Phi$ is the cumulative distribution function of the normal distribution. The estimation of the model yields results that can be used to predict the probability that an industry is contained in a specific city. In the second stage, the initial model is estimated by OLS with the dependent variable of continuous productivity growth, which corrects the selection bias by incorporating the variable called the Mills inverse ratio ($\lambda$), which is derived from the previous stage.

### 3.3 Endogeneity and instrumental variables

When estimating the impact of agglomeration economies on local results such as productivity growth, the literature recognizes two potential sources of endogeneity: omitted variables and inverse causality. Either may arise at the local and individual level (Combes, Gobillon 2015), and their treatment focuses on instrumental variables, including historical and geographical variables, for each endogenous regressor, specialization, diversity, and density.

According to Combes, Gobillon (2015), historical values of population or density are relevant, because by remaining in time, they create inertia in the population and in local economic activity. This idea is imputed to the construction of the instruments for the variables of specialization and diversity. For that reason, the instruments are generated from the data of the birth of firms. The birth of firms is considered correlated with the level of specialization and diversity of the industries in the cities, but not directly with the growth of employment and productivity. The dummy of geological character is related to all the endogenous variables and does not represent a direct effect on the variables of interest or the geographical variables related to the availability of roads in 1980, also generated as dummies.

Estimating the effect of location, urbanization economies, and density on productivity using instrumental variables can lead to unbiased estimates, provided that the instruments meet the conditions of relevance (7) and exogeneity (8). Formally, these conditions are:

$$\begin{aligned}
Cov(Specialization_a, Z_a|.) &\neq 0 \\
Cov(Diversity_a, Z_a|.) &\neq 0 \\
Cov(Density_a, Z_a|.) &\neq 0
\end{aligned} \tag{7}$$

$$\begin{aligned}
Cov(\mu_a^x, Z_a) &= 0 \\
\text{for } x &= \text{productivity}
\end{aligned} \tag{8}$$

$Z$ denotes the set of instruments.

Equation (7) denotes that the relevance of an instrument depends on the partial correlation of the instrumental variables and the endogenous regressors. These are obtained by Ordinary Least Squares (OLS) estimates for each endogenous regressor of the growth of productivity in instrumental variables, including regional, provincial, and industrial fixed effects. The results show that the relevant instruments for specialization are the specialization index, the population density of 1950, the urbanization index of 1980, the availability of roads in 1980, and a geological dummy. For the diversity and density of employment these same instruments are relevant, except the specialization index.

The analysis of the relevance of the defined instruments is validated by the test developed by Stock, Yogo (2005)[2], who define two tests for weak instruments based on a single $F$ statistic. The values in all cases are greater than $10^3$, suggesting that the instruments are strong; their strength is confirmed when they contradict the critical values reported by Stock, Yogo (2005).

The condition of exogeneity suggested in equation (8), that is, the orthogonality with respect to the error term, is evaluated with the Sargan over-identification test, which allows us to reject the hypothesis of restriction of over-identification, suggesting the joint exogeneity of the instruments.

## 4   Estimation and analysis

The model specified to estimate the effect of agglomeration economies on the productivity growth of a particular industry in a certain canton between 1980 and 2010 appears below. In particular, the Two-Stage Least Squares (2SLS) estimator is used due to the aforementioned aspects of endogeneity, focused on regressions with instrumental variables.

$$\Delta prod_{ic} = \beta_0 + \beta_1 \log spe_{ic} + \beta_2 \log div_{ic} + \beta_3 size_{ic} + \beta_4 den_c + imr_{-e} + imr_{-p} + \varepsilon_{ic} \quad (9)$$

where $\Delta prod_{ic}$ represents the growth of productivity in industry $i$ and city $c$ between both years, respectively; $spe_{ic}$, $div_{ic}$, $size_{ic}$ are the indices of specialization, diversity, and average industry size $i$ in city $c$; and $den_c$ is the density of total employment. The variables $imr_{-e}$ and $imr_{-p}$ are the inverse ratio of Mills for employment and productivity in each case, introduced to control the selection bias, and $\varepsilon_{ic}$ is assumed as the error term. To control for unobservable heterogeneity, we introduce fixed effects at the province, industry, and regional[4] levels. The literacy rate of each city aims to capture the qualifications of the population in each case[5].

The explanatory variables correspond to the initial year, 1980, and have been normalized by the corresponding values at the national level. All the variables are expressed in logarithms, which is why the estimated parameters are their elasticities with respect to each variable. This makes them easily comparable and interpretable.

The first estimates of equation (9) are made by OLS. However, given the presence of selection bias and the endogeneity of the model, such results are not entirely correct, as it is pertinent to apply two additional estimation strategies. To correct the selection bias, we proceeded with maximum likelihood estimations through a Tobit Type II model, while the endogeneity of the model implies estimations with instrumental variables (2SLS) with results accepted as definitive (Table 2).

As a robustness test, a strategy for estimating productivity growth is applied that is less sensitive to weak instruments: the limited information maximum likelihood (LIML)

---

[2]Stock, Yogo (2005) provide two tests that, based on the F statistic, have two purposes. The first is to test the hypothesis that in small samples the bias in the 2SLS regressions is small with respect to the endogeneity bias reported by MCO ("bias test"). The second is to use the Wald test to determine whether an instrument is considered strong, that is, that its size is close to its level for all possible configurations of the regression by instrumental variables ("size test"). Therefore, the instruments may be weak in one sense but not in another.

[3]Cameron, Trivedi (2010) indicate that a measure widely used by Staiger, Stock (1997), that is, $F < 10$, suggests weak instruments.

[4]In Ecuador, there are three natural regions: Coast, Highland, and Amazonian regions.

[5]No data is available on the qualification of employees by industry and city.

Table 2: Productivity growth: Estimates by OLS, Tobit and IV

| Productivity | OLS | TOBIT | 2SLS |
|---|---|---|---|
| specialization | -0.075* | 0.091 | -0.285 |
|  | (0.026) | (0.073) | (0.166) |
| diversity | 0.064 | -0.189 | 0.397* |
|  | (0.046) | (0.178) | (0.183) |
| density | 0.031 | -0.019 | -0.161* |
|  | (0.019) | (0.043) | (0.081) |
| size firms | -0.021 | 0.229* | 0.049 |
|  | (0.036) | (0.101) | (0.077) |
| inverse Mills ratio | -0.032 |  | -0.767 |
|  | (0.119) |  | (0.341) |
| N | 2963 | 2963 | 2963 |
| F | — | — | 14.75 |
| CONTROL |  |  |  |
| Literacy index 1980 | Yes | — | Yes |
| FIXED EFFECTS |  |  |  |
| Region | Yes | No | Yes |
| Province | Yes | No | Yes |
| Industry | Yes | Yes | Yes |
| Over identificaction (Sargan Test) | — | — | 1.145 |
| P value - SarganTest | — | — | (0.5640) |

*Notes*: Standard errors in parentheses. P-values: * $p < 0.1$, ** $p < 0.05$, *** $p < 0.01$. All variables are expressed in logarithms.

estimator. This strategy takes into account only the likelihood function of the endogenous variables of equation (9) and the identification of restrictions corresponding to the equation to be estimated.

The results obtained are supported with those obtained by 2SLS and are consistent with previous empirical findings given that the productivity gains of urban agglomeration economies are generally found to be positive (Melo et al. 2009), The results obtained differ in that the location economies are not significant. At this point, it should be noted that 94% of the firms of the two years analyzed correspond to the category of microenterprise, 4% correspond to small firms, and the 2% remaining percentage are medium and large firms[6]. This corresponds to the finding of Jacobs (1969) that small businesses benefit more from urban diversity in large cities due to their greater dependence on external industrial environments for multiple intermediate inputs, while large companies are self-sufficient.

## 5   Conclusion

In particular, two different contributions to the literature are presented. The first relates to the agglomeration literature about Latin American countries like Ecuador that have received little attention from this approach.

The growth of productivity is determined significantly and positively by urbanization economies, while the density elasticity is negative. This is interpreted as the result of the effects of congestion. These results are consistent with other works for developed countries Cingano, Schivardi (2004) and Guevara et al. (2015) for Ecuador. They approximate labor productivity in 2010, both in industry and in services, as a function of specialization, diversity, competence, and density (of firms or employment) in the cities of Ecuador. Using as main instruments the spatial delays of each of the endogenous variables, their results suggest a strong positive externality of the diversity in the productivity of the

---

[6]In Ecuador, companies are classified as micro, small, medium, and large depending on whether they have between 1 and 9, 10-49, 50-199, or more than 200 employees, respectively.

manufacturing industries (1,651) and of the services (2,081). In manufacturing, the density of employment is also statistically significant.

Productivity takes place in provincial capitals, characterized by the concentration of public sector intervention, both in terms of investments (public goods) and public consumption (services); ease of access to large markets; and the possibility of finding large niches of specialization, and access to a broad labor market and specialized urban functions.

Second, in terms of Ecuador's public policy, a boost to industry and services is expected within the framework of the country's industrial policy. For the period 2016-2025, this policy aims to generate 251,000 new jobs; to invest 13,600 million dollars; contribute positively to the trade balance of 1,200 million dollars; and increase GDP by 10 percentage points. Ecuador's public policy recognizes the imminent change in the spatial distribution of economic activities and that it is necessary to focus on land use and labor mobility relating to trade in intermediate goods. Consequently, the industrial policy must mesh with others that consider the spatial dimension. In the area of externalities in particular, the challenge is to balance negative externalities and exploit the positive externalities of agglomeration based on greater knowledge, an important mechanism through which the agglomeration economies act.

## References


Arrow K (1962) The economic implications of learning by doing. *Review of Economics and Statistics* 29: 155–173

Cameron AC, Trivedi PK (2010) *Microeconometrics Using Stata* (Revised ed.). Stata Press, College Station, TX

Cingano F, Schivardi F (2004) Identifying the sources of local productivity growth. *Journal of the European Economic Association* 2[4]: 720–744. CrossRef.

Combes P, Gobillon L (2015) The empirics of agglomeration economies. In: Duranton G, Henderson V, Strange W (eds), *Handbook of Regional and Urban Economics*, Volume 5. North Holland, Amsterdam, 247–348

Combes PP (2000) Economic structure and local growth: France, 1984-1993. *Journal of urban economics* 47[3]: 329–355

Glaeser E, Kallal H, Scheinkman J, Shleifer A (1992) Growth in cities. *Journal of Political Economy* 100[6]: 1126–1152. CrossRef.

Guevara C, Riou S, Autant-Bernard C (2015) Agglomeration externalities and urbanization in Ecuador. 55th congress of the European Regional Science Association, Lisbon, Portugal, https://halshs.archives-ouvertes.fr/halshs-01212174

Heckman J (1979) Sample selection bias as a specification error. *Econometrica* 47[1]: 153–161

Henderson J, Kuncoro A, Turner M (1995) Industrial development in cities. *Journal of Political Economy* 103[5]: 1067–1090. CrossRef.

Jacobs J (1969) *The Economy of Cities*. Random House, New York

Marshall A (1890) *Principles of Economic*. MacMillan, London

Melo PC, Graham DJ, Noland RB (2009) A meta-analysis of estimates of urban agglomeration economies. *Regional Science and Urban Economics* 39[3]: 332–342. CrossRef.

Romer P (1986) Increasing returns and long-run growth. *Journal of Political Economy* 94: 1002–1037

Staiger D, Stock J (1997) Instrumental variables regression with weak instruments. *Econometrica* 65: 557–586

Stock J, Yogo M (2005) Testing for weak instruments in linear iv regression. In: Andrews D, Stock J (eds), *Identification and Inference in Econometric Models: Essays in Honor of Thomas J. Rothenberg*. Cambridge University Press, Cambridge, UK, Chapter 5

Viladecans-Marsal E (2004) Agglomeration economies and industrial location: City-level evidence. *Journal of Economic Geography* 4[5]: 565–582. CrossRef.

Volume 5, Number 3, 2018, 49–73
DOI: 10.18335/region.v5i3.224

journal homepage: region.ersa.org

# Governance of metropolitan areas for delivery of public services in Latin America: the cases of Bogota, Lima and Mexico City

Alejandra Berenice Trejo Nieto[1], José Luis Niño Amezquita[2], María Luisa Vasquez[3]

[1] El Colegio de México, Mexico City, Mexico
[2] CREPIB, Tunja, Colombia
[3] Independent consultant, Lima, Peru

Received: 29 November 2017/Accepted: 16 October 2018

**Abstract.** One of the key issues at metropolitan level is the provision of public services and this paper highlights the importance of understanding the governance of public services in the context of increasing urbanization and decentralization. This paper provides a comparative analysis on metropolitan governance in Latin America by analysing specific case studies. The objective is to identify how the governance setting in metropolitan areas shapes the process and the results of providing public services to wider population. We examine metropolitan governance by employing a 3x3x3 model as a framework for addressing key issues about urban services delivery. Bogota, Lima and Mexico City are the metropolitan areas selected. Secondly, we focus on three sectors: transport, solid waste collection and water. Finally, the analysis focuses in three aspects of governance: coordination, financial sustainability and coverage and quality. The data collection process involved field research in Bogota, Lima and Mexico City.

## 1 Introduction

The urban transition in Latin America throughout the twentieth century was relatively rapid, and the move to urban living continues at an accelerated pace in several countries in the region. One of the most striking recent features of urbanization in Latin America has been the emergence of metropolitan areas: cities that have surpassed the limits of their immediate outermost periphery, expanding beyond their administrative boundaries. In some cases, urbanization and urban expansion have led to the emergence of megacities that are national centers of economic or political power, such as Sao Paulo and Mexico City. Metropolitan areas face significant economic, social, political and environmental challenges that extend beyond the borders of local governments, including different administrative divisions across the territory. The provision of public services has become one of the most critical and pressing metropolitan concerns. While the theory and praxis of providing services in metropolitan areas have been subjects of great interest in advanced countries, they have been largely downplayed in low- and middle-income countries (Bahl 2013). Furthermore, some normative discussions about metropolitan areas in Latin America have focused on ideal government models, yet there is very little in the existing literature on the problems of providing public services at the metropolitan level. This paper highlights the importance of knowing and understanding how public services are provided in the context of increasing metropolitanization and decentralization due to the hypothesized negative impact of politico-administrative fragmentation. According to some studies, fragmentation translates into weak governance, creating substantial difficulties in providing services. Despite this predominant assumption, the body of knowledge on the key governance challenges in metropolitan areas, especially in less developed countries, is not robust and lacks empirical work and comparative studies. This study contributes to the literature by implementing a comparative analysis of public service provision in metropolitan areas in Latin America.

Our general research question refers to the characteristics and outcomes of governance for delivering public services in metropolitan areas, and how, in practice, governance schemes accommodate different contexts. More specifically, the paper deals with the following questions: What are the underlying characteristics of metropolitan governance and organization in Latin American countries? How do metropolitan areas organize the provision of public services? What is the performance of services delivery in terms of financial sustainability, coverage and quality? How do governance and outcomes vary across different services and metropolitan areas?

We employed a 3x3x3 model of comparative analysis with three metropolitan areas (Bogota, Lima, and Mexico City), three services (public transport, solid waste collection, and piped water), and three aspects of governance (coverage and quality, financial sustainability, and coordination). Analyzing the provision of public services in different metropolitan areas in the Latin American region, we discuss how variation in metropolitan organization translates into specific outcomes across the selected cases. A variety of governance structures are identified, a few of which attempt to reverse some of the negative effects of jurisdictional fragmentation. The collected data includes secondary sources (statistics, reports, and documents), and field research in Bogota, Lima, and Mexico City, where a number of focus groups, interviews and technical visits took place. The paper includes a synthetic literature review, a description of the methodological design, an overview of the metropolitan organization and structures in the three selected areas, the research results and discussion. We conclude with a number of final remarks that can be useful for metropolitan level public policies.

## 2   Metropolitan Governance and Provision of Local Public Services

Metropolitan areas are huge and complex urban areas whose functional scope extends beyond their jurisdictional boundaries. There is commonly political-administrative fragmentation, and policy implementation resides with individual autonomous local authorities. This is a challenge for urban planning, management and policy design. Because of their scale, complexity and fixed government structures, metropolitan areas conduct their planning and policy tasks in difficult environments. Metropolitan areas must provide services and infrastructure in sophisticated ways because the structure of land use is more diverse, the magnitude and complexity of expenditure is much greater, and the size and concentration of the population is larger than in other urban areas (Slack 2007). One of the key areas of public action at the metropolitan level is the provision of services. As metropolitan areas extend to multiple local jurisdictions, there is an increasing need to expand service provision to fulfill the population's social needs. Inadequate provision of basic services translates into significant gaps between demand for and supply of urban services. Large intra-urban disparities can develop. Given the intricacy of metropolitan areas, governance plays an important role in the effective delivery of services. Governance defines the quantity and quality of services provided, their efficiency, and their equitable cost sharing (Jones et al. 2014, Slack 2007, Bird, Slack 2007).

The long-standing debate on how to govern and manage metropolitan areas, whether via decentralized or consolidated structures, has been framed mostly in the theoretical discussion around government decentralization and its consequences for efficiency and equity (Bird, Slack 2007, p. 730). According to the subsidiarity principle, subnational levels of government achieve greater welfare gains by adjusting the provision of public goods and services to citizens' preferences and local costs (Oates 1997). Decentralization favors accountability, and horizontal competition triggers a better supply of public goods (Tiebout 1956). On the other hand, consolidation facilitates the exploitation of economies of scale, the management of externalities, and the quest for equity (Treisman 2000). Consolidation can also contribute to minimizing the dangers of elite capture and corruption, especially in developing countries (Prud'homme 1995).

Echoing the principles above, the Public Choice School argues that decentralized metropolitan governments spur effective and efficient service delivery by promoting competition (Yaro, Ronderos 2011), whereas Regionalism and New Consolidationist supporters argue in favor of metropolitan governments (Lowery 2000). In practice a variety of metropolitan structures have been implemented, based either on the fragmented version or on different forms of government consolidation. Slack (2007) and Bird, Slack (2007), for instance, identify the one-tier fragmented model, the single-tier consolidated model, the two-tier model, and the one-tier model with voluntary cooperation.

According to Storper (2014), fragmentation is an inevitable condition in metropolitan areas, and the regulation of the resulting interdependent relations in the absence of an overarching political authority is highly problematic. The enduring gaps between functional and administrative boundaries mean that there will always be governance problems at hand, and neither complete consolidation nor fragmentation is likely to resolve these fundamental metropolitan issues. Rather than a single government, metropolitan areas require structures of governance that are sufficiently open to allow for diverse solutions in an environment characterized by variable conditions (Parks, Oakerson 1989). Following Parks, Oakerson (1989), jurisdictionally fragmented metropolitan areas are complexly organized. However, organizational diversity and complexity do not necessarily imply institutional failure and can in fact lead to higher efficiency. By means of agreements and associations, local governments, civil society, and the private sector acting together in a coordinated manner can achieve acceptable governance structures (Feiock 2004). Therefore, there is no single correct way to organize metropolitan areas, and no single geography or organization of governance, and arrangements for service provision are place- and time-specific (Bahl 2013, Slack 2007, Parks, Oakerson 1993, 1989). In the particular case of public services, efficient scales and preferences can be multiple and heterogeneous, and evolve over time (Slack 2007, Parks, Oakerson 1989). Public services also have diverse production functions and financial and cost structures (Parks, Oakerson 1989).

The fundamental distinction between the provision and the production of public services makes the case for organizational structures that allow for a more complete depiction of metropolitan governance and its complexity. Local governments are provision units that use a variety of alternative production arrangements: direct production, private contracting, coordinated or joint production, or franchising. Therefore, metropolitan areas comprise multiple provision units that are linked in numerous ways to a variety of production units. This variety usually represents rational accommodations to diversity. The choice of governance arrangements is contingent upon a multiplicity of environmental factors, yet governance depends, above all, on the capacity to elaborate on, change and enforce the rules within which provision and production occur (Parks, Oakerson 1989). Governance structures can transcend municipal boundaries and allow problem solving, rule making and efficiency on a metropolitan basis. However, when close voluntary organization and cooperation are not achieved, metropolitan governance weakens (Parks, Oakerson 1993). Accordingly, the different levels of governance (provision and production arrangements and the sets of rules and institutions) are what matter (Figure 1).

## 3    Methodological Framework and Data Collection

As a methodological strategy for this research we employed a comparative case study analysis implemented by means of a 3x3x3 model. The first 3 in the model refers to the selected metropolises, the second indicates the number of services and the third relates to specific aspects of governance (Figure 2). This approach is a useful starting point for an international and comparative analysis of metropolitan governance in the highly-urbanized countries of Latin America with its varying city sizes, metropolitan structures, and outcomes.

The metropolitan areas of Bogota, Lima, and Mexico City are the subjects of this

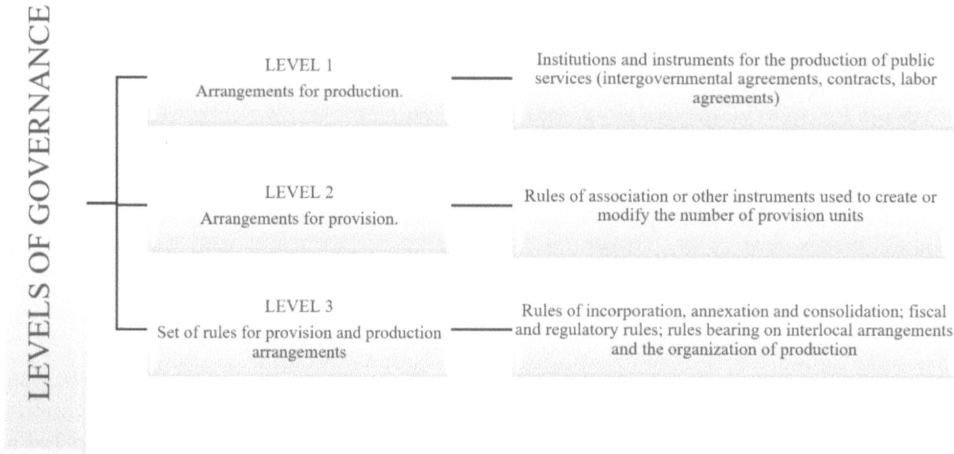


*Source*: Authors' elaboration based on Parks, Oakerson (1993)

Figure 1: Metropolitan governance organization

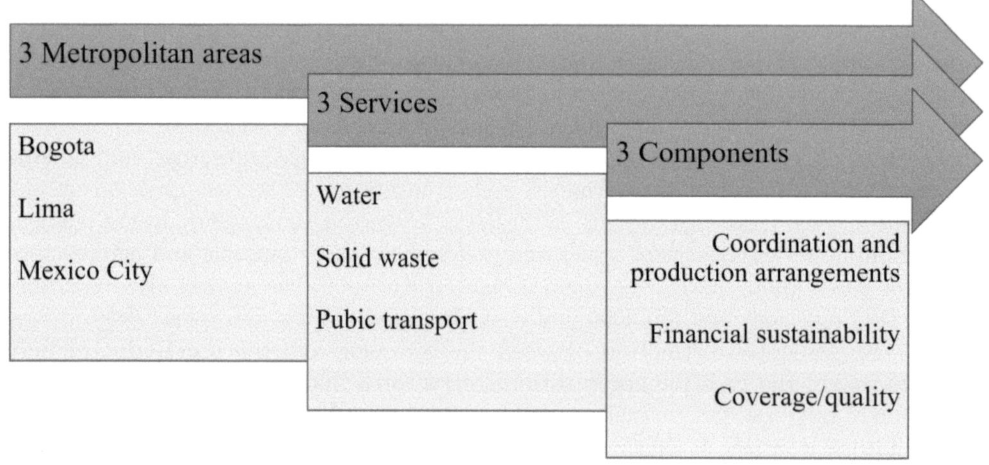


*Source*: Authors' elaboration

Figure 2: Components of the 3 x 3 x 3 model of analysis

analysis. All three metropolitan areas have undergone processes of rapid metropolization which have engendered important challenges for the provision of public services and infrastructure. They all belong to the Latin American region and have some cultural background and colonial roots in common. The three metropolitan areas are capital cities that have special political-administrative status. Even though their countries operate under different political systems, with unitary governments in Colombia and Peru, and a federal government in Mexico, they have undertaken important decentralization processes. These metropolitan areas also offer the possibility of illustrating variability in governance structures. In addition, they present different historical forms of metropolitan expansion and institutionalization.

Although the number of public services provided in metropolitan areas is extensive, we focus on three of the most critical sectors in the urban context that are generally provided at the local level: transport, solid waste collection, and water. These sectors are strategic in urban planning and affect the day-to-day life of the population. Moreover, they denote the kinds of service that pose unique challenges in metropolitan environments (Boex et al. 2013, Jones et al. 2014). Jones et al. (2014) suggest that governance plays an important role in the effective delivery of services in urban areas through coordination mechanisms, finances, and technical operation. This analysis includes these three areas: coordination and production arrangements; financial sustainability; and service coverage and quality. Given the scope of this project, the analysis does not include elements such as civil society participation, transparency, and accountability.

The data collection process included desktop and field work. Documental and secondary statistical information from international, national and local sources was gathered. The results and discussion in this paper also rely on the data collected during the fieldwork period. In 2016, we conducted field research in the three selected cities and organized a final seminar and a conference in Mexico City. The fieldwork included workshops, interviews and technical visits. Nine workshops were organized: one for each sector (transportation, water, and waste collection) in each city. The participants at these workshops were actors or experts in the governance of public service provision: the academic sector, civil society, local government and private suppliers. We located sources of potential participants based on their location and willingness to participate. The workshops were designed as small focus groups where participants reported on and discussed the situation and the challenges to each public service that different actors perceived at the metropolitan level. There was a number of guiding questions about the three categories of analysis, and we allowed other issues to emerge (see the guiding questionnaire and participants in the methodological appendix). The workshops lasted approximately two hours each, and took place in small auditoriums.

Furthermore, twelve semi-structured interviews were carried out. The sample universe was composed of local authorities such as municipal mayors or specific local officials (in the urban services area), community leaders, and sector-specific managers or providers who were unable to participate in the workshops but were relevant actors in some area of urban public services. Although this was a small-scale interview project, it provided enough scope for identifying and developing cross-case evidence rather than generalities. We assessed the adequacy of the sample in terms not of size, but of the sample's ability to supply key information needed for the analysis.

Six technical visits to the metropolitan peripheries were incorporated as part of the field research. Due to time and budget constraints the number of technical visits was restricted. The criteria for choosing a location were access to some local informants, a big and a small municipality outside the central city, and the presence of important formal or informal housing development expansion. The assumption was that these municipalities would experience emerging and persistent governance issues. Technical visits involved observation, interviews and informal conversations with residents. The results were presented and discussed at the final seminar.

Based on analysis of the transcripts and reports on the interviews, visits and workshops, major issues were identified and reported. A contextual characterization of the governance of each metropolitan area was developed. This was followed by an analysis based on the different services (transport, solid waste collection and water). The comparative approach allowed us to evaluate variations across metropolitan areas and services. This paper's size limit precludes a full in-depth analysis of each case; nonetheless, valuable findings are discussed for an initial assessment of metropolitan governance.

## 4   Overview of Metropolitan Structures in Mexico City, Lima and Bogota

On a larger scale, Latin American cities are expanding rapidly and frequently faster than population growth elsewhere in the country. The result has been the emergence of urban areas of a large territorial size comprising multiple jurisdictions. Alongside territorial and functional restructuring, metropolitan areas have faced political decentralization aimed at producing new spaces for participation, reducing fiscal imbalance problems, and organizing the local and territorial levels of the State in order to implement social policies and deliver services efficiently. Despite these generalized trends, metropolitan areas in each country have highly diverse features. This section presents background on the institutional and territorial structures in the metropolitan areas of Mexico City, Lima and Bogota.

*Source*: Authors' elaboration

Figure 3: Mexico City Metropolitan Area

### 4.1  Mexico City Metropolitan Area

Mexico City Metropolitan Area (MCMA), one of the largest metropolitan areas in the world, is the result of the explosive growth and expansion of the urban center during the twentieth century. Due to the displacement of industrial activity and housing towards the periphery, the city began its expansion into other jurisdictions outside its administrative boundaries in the 1940s (Trejo 2013). At the time of the 2010 Population Census, MCMA comprised over 20 million inhabitants, and had a land size of almost 8,000 square kilometers and an average population density of 2,557 inhabitants per square kilometer (SEDESOL et al. 2012). In 2013, MCMA accounted for 18% of the national population and around 25% of total gross domestic product.

MCMA includes the administrative area of Mexico City[1], formerly called the Federal District, 59 adjacent municipalities in the State of Mexico, and a municipality in the state of Hidalgo (Figure 3). Mexico City proper, itself composed of 16 boroughs, is the political and economic seat of power. Prior to the approval of a political reform in 2015, it was governed by special statute. In contrast to states, it did not have full autonomy, and until 1997 its head of government was not elected directly by the inhabitants, but appointed by the President. Furthermore, the head of government had no constitutional or regulatory capacity and boroughs had neither the autonomy nor all the functions of municipalities.

Metropolitan areas in Mexico do not have legal status as official jurisdictions, but the constitution allows intermunicipal cooperation on a voluntary basis. Several governments operate on different levels, leading to the evolution of different and frequently clashing policies and rules. The administrative powers of 60 municipalities overlap with the government of Mexico City, which in turn interacts with the powers of two different states, Mexico and Hidalgo, as well as with the power of the central government (Figure 4). Politico-administrative fragmentation, measured as the number of jurisdictions with more than 100,000 inhabitants, indicates that 39 municipalities and boroughs have populations of over that figure. This fragmentation decreases if we consider Mexico City proper as a single local government (24 jurisdictions with populations of over 100,000 inhabitants).

Legal planning, coordination and political structures have not been conducive to metropolitan-scale organization. Attempts at constructing effective metropolitan agreements and commissions have been largely ineffective, due to the lack of financial, regulatory and decision-making authority (Cenizal 2015)[2]. Thus MCMA entails a complex set of

---

[1]Mexico City proper.

[2]Article 115 in the Mexican Constitution allows for the coordination of states and municipalities to address urban problems. Two or more municipalities and their respective states are also allowed to create a conurbation commission. Article 122 allows cooperation between Mexico City and its neighboring municipalities.

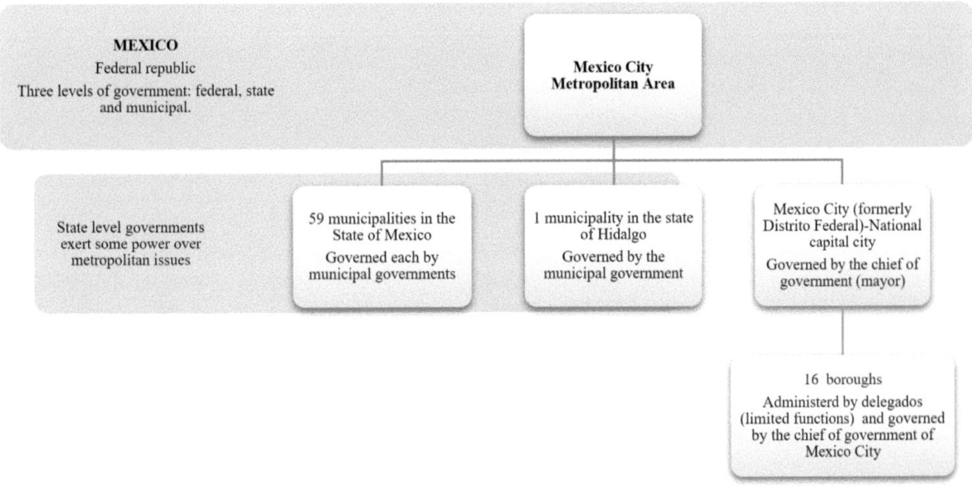


*Source*: Authors' elaboration

Figure 4: Government structure, Mexico City Metropolitan Area

governmental entities with overlapping federal, state, and local powers and an intricate organizational structure that complicates metropolitan governance arrangements, in particular planning schemes seeking to deliver services efficiently (Perlman et al. 2011).

## 4.2 Lima

The Metropolitan Area of Lima includes the provinces of Lima and Callao. In the province of Lima, the metropolitan municipality assumes the functions of both regional government and provincial municipality. In the province of Callao, regional and provincial government are separate; this means that the Regional Government of Callao and the Provincial Municipality of Callao exercise their respective functions over the same jurisdiction. The province of Lima covers 49 districts governed by 48 district municipalities, whereas the capital district is governed by the Metropolitan Municipality of Lima. In turn, the Province of Callao has seven districts governed by six district municipalities, and the capital district of Callao is governed by the Provincial Municipality of Callao (Figure 5). The population has grown rapidly since the mid-twentieth century. In 1940, Lima and Callao had a population of 645,000 inhabitants; in 1972 this had risen to over three million, and in 1993 it was over six million. In the 1970s the two provinces became a conurbation (Figure 6). In 2013, the population was 9,752,000, of which one million were in Callao (INEI 2014). A total of 25 of the 49 districts have a population of over 100,000.

Lima not only has special arrangements as a capital district; it also has been treated differentially in the decentralization process. While other regional governments, including the regional government of Callao, have taken on functions such as health and education, the process has been discriminatory against the Metropolitan Municipality of Lima, where central government remains the provider of various public services (Diálogos de Políticas Pública 2015). The Organic Law of Municipalities allows the use of coordination mechanisms between municipalities to ensure the efficient use of public resources. Municipalities can create associations with other municipalities called mancomunidades. In order to provide services and implement joint infrastructure projects, seven such associations have been created. They have developed efforts to coordinate and provide services in security and waste management[3]. However, mechanisms for coordination between the municipalities of Lima and Callao have been weakly implemented.

---

[3]http://www.limacomovamos.org/boletines/las-7-mancomunidades-de-lima/#!prettyPhoto[inline]/-0/

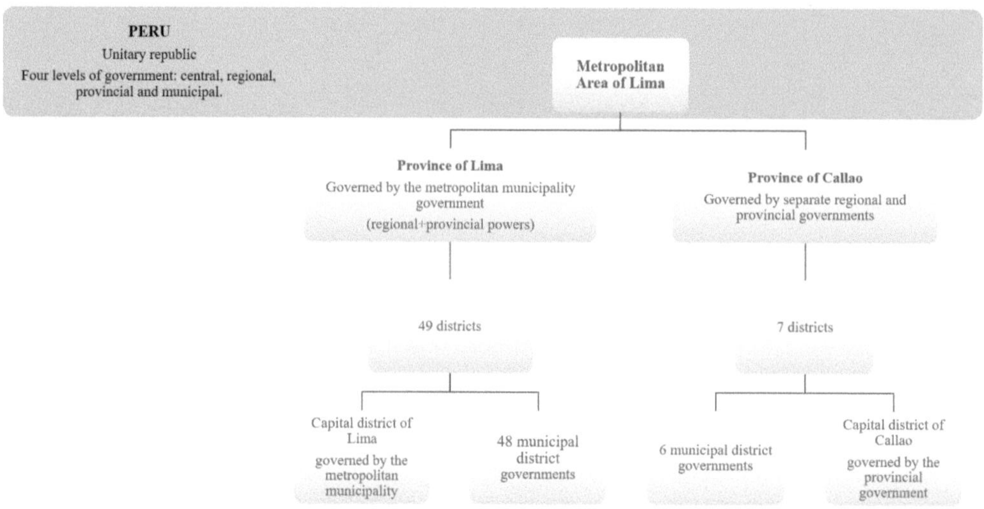


*Source*: Authors' elaboration

Figure 5: Government structure, Metropolitan Area of Lima

### 4.3 Bogota

According to the National Administrative Department of Statistics (DANE 2017) the Metropolitan Area of Bogota includes Bogota District and the municipalities of Bojacá, Cajicá, Chía, Cogua, Cota, El Rosal, Facatatíva, Funza, Gachancipá, La Calera, Madrid, Mosquera, Nemocón, Soacha, Sibaté, Sopó, Subachoque, Tabio, Tenjo, Tocancipá and Zipacón (Figure 7). It had a population of 7.8 million inhabitants in 2005 rising to 9.3 million in 2015[4], making Bogota the largest metropolitan area in Colombia, one of the largest in South America, and one of the 33 most-populated metropolises in the world (Smith 2014). The Bogota District was the product of Decree 3640, approved in 1954, which annexed the surrounding municipalities of Engativá, Fontibón, Suba, Usme, Usaquén and Bosa through the Seventh Ordinance of the Administrative Council of Cundinamarca. The territory of Sumapaz was annexed in 1955. According to Article 199 of the 1986 political constitution, administration of the district is the responsibility of the municipal council. Therefore, the city of Bogota is organized as a special district, without subjection to the ordinary municipal regime, under the conditions fixed by the law. With the approval of the Colombian political Constitution of 1991, Bogota became a Capital District with special status. The new Constitution, which includes an Organic Statute for Bogota, redefines the Capital District and eliminates the concept of annexed municipalities to introduce the concept of localities.

The Organic Law of Territorial Ordering sets the principles of good governance in the metropolitan area. This law recognizes that metropolitan areas are territorial associative schemes and that the national government should promote metropolitan cooperation. Article 15 allows associations between metropolitan areas. These can take place between two or more metropolitan areas to jointly organize the provision of public services, the implementation of regional projects, and the fulfillment of administrative functions. Such projects may be developed through contracts, agreements or plans. There are also municipal associative bodies, as in the case of Savannah Centro and Northern Savanna and an agreement of cities in the periphery. Although the Bogota metropolitan area is fragmented, unlike in Mexico City and Lima the dynamics of the metropolitan area are strongly concentrated in Bogota District (Figure 8).

---

[4]For more information about the census in the metropolitan area: http://www.dane.gov.co/files/-censo2005/resultados_am_municipios.pdf

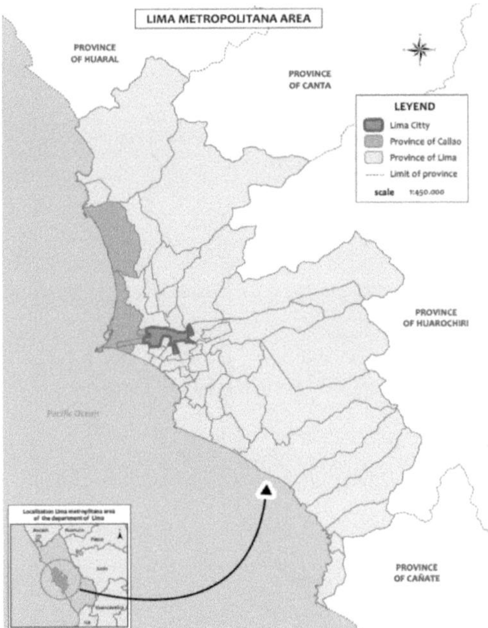



*Source*: Authors' elaboration

Figure 6: Metropolitan Area of Lima

## 5 Metropolitan Governance of Public Services: An exploratory examination

In this section we analyze the governance structures in place in our three metropolitan areas according to the explicit and implicit constituent elements of service supply. The main findings regarding coordination, financial sustainability and coverage/quality are discussed. Considering the issue of coordination contributes to understanding governance organization, whereas looking at the financial aspects and coverage help to illustrate efficiency and equity. The approach suggested by Parks, Oakerson (1993) and summarized in Figure 1 is a useful guiding scheme to identify the different arrangements and levels of metropolitan governance that operate in each service and metropolitan area: arrangements for production (level 1), arrangements for provision (level 2) and the set of rules for production and provision (level 3).

### 5.1 Waste collection

Each metropolitan area has a more or less complex governance organization and operation depending on the diversity of actors involved in its regulation, management and production. According to Article 115 of the Mexican Constitution, solid waste management is provided by the municipalities. In Mexico City proper each borough must provide the service (level 2). Three schemes of production are: public; private; and public-private (level 1). In some boroughs, participatory budgeting projects for local waste collection is a supplementary formal mechanism for providing the service. In both the State of Mexico and Mexico City proper there is a large informal sector (waste pickers, burreros -pickers that use donkeys to transport waste- or carretoneros -pickers that transport waste by carts-) who have historically had strong unions and powerful leaders. Some municipalities have a Councilman (regidor) and in municipalities with greater organizational complexity there is a Director of Public Services. Regarding level 3 of governance – where the rules for provision and production arrangements for service delivery are made – the government of the State of Mexico formulates waste management policy through the Ministry of Environment. In Mexico City proper the Ministry of the Interior, the Ministry of Works and Services through its General Directorate of Urban Services, the Ministry of the Environment and the Environmental Attorney of Land Management participate in urban solid waste regulation and management.

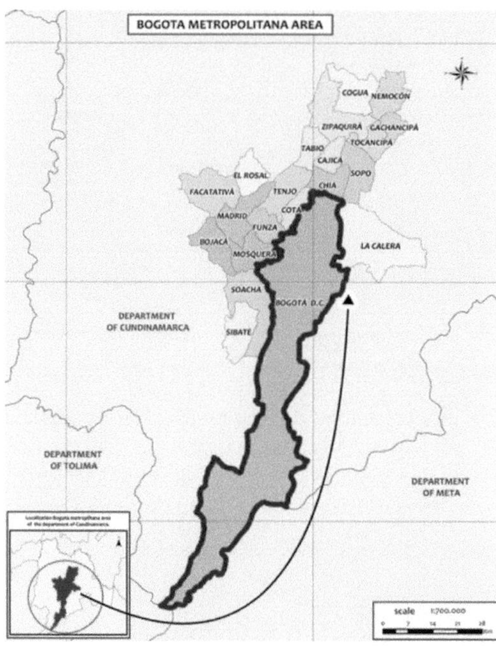



*Source*: DIRNI, recovered by Mayor of Bogota (2015)

Figure 7: Metropolitan area of Bogota according to DANE (2005 census)

In Lima, provincial municipalities are responsible for waste disposal whereas district municipalities are in charge of the collection and transportation of solid waste. In the capital districts of Lima and Callao, the provincial municipalities are responsible for the collection and transport of solid waste (Durand 2012). Service provision operates under a two-tier arrangement throughout fifty districts and two provinces (level 2). Cleaning and waste collection are supplied directly by municipalities or by private companies contracted to municipalities (level 1). Two large private companies, Petramas and Innova Ambiental, provide the service for several municipalities. There are also municipalities with mixed production schemes. Provincial municipalities regulate the disposal of solid, liquid and industrial discharge. The Metropolitan Municipality of Lima has a special legal regime with special functions in sanitation. It organizes the Metropolitan System of Solid Waste Treatment and Disposal, signs concession contracts for waste management services, and controls their operation. The district municipalities decide on areas for landfill and waste accumulation (Organic Law of Municipalities Nr 27972). The Ministry of Health's General Directorate of Environmental Health controls landfill and authorizes the work of companies that collect municipal waste. The Direction of Environmental Quality formulates national policy on solid waste management; however, it conducts waste management policy with limited normative prerogatives (level 3) (Durand 2012).

According to Law 142, normative control of the waste collection service in Colombia is the responsibility of the National Regulatory Committee for Drinking Water and Basic Sanitation, which regulates competition between service providers to avoid monopolies. The National Superintendence of Domestic Utility Services controls and inspects the efficiency of the service. There is a Municipal Special Administrative Unit of Public Utilities which directs, controls and supervises the provision of road-cleaning services and the collection and final placement of solid waste. The District Department of Environment regulates and promotes environmental sustainability. Lastly, the municipal intercapital consortium supervises the administrative, technical, operative, commercial, economic, and financial aspects of solid waste management and collection (level 3) (Ciudad Limpia 2017). The service is provided by Bogota Capital District and the rest of the municipalities (level 2). In recent years, Bogota's solid waste service has been supplied by the Water Company. There are also other companies involved, such as Ciudad Limpia, which deals with waste in Bosa and Kennedy, and a number of recycling companies that collect, transport, and

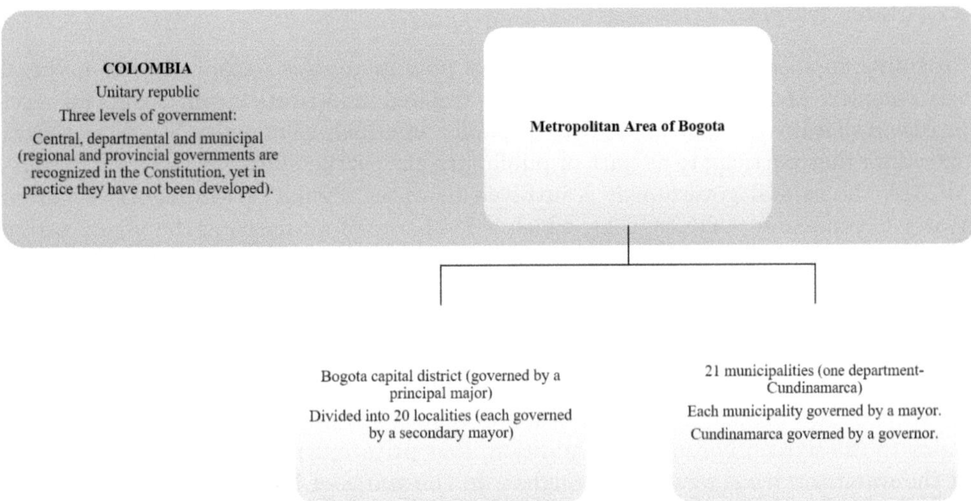


*Source*: Authors' elaboration

Figure 8: Government structure, Metropolitan Area of Bogota

separate, where appropriate, solid waste. The city administration has implemented a new sanitary scheme which assigns five areas of service to five private enterprises (level 1).

Coordination is weak or altogether lacking, depending on the city. In Bogota there is no horizontal coordination between Soacha and Bogota, but service providers and recyclers cooperate at the local level. In Lima, incipient horizontal coordination is sought through the formation of associations of municipalities, but Callao is excluded. Provision and production in MCMA lack mechanisms for coordination between boroughs and municipalities.

In Bogota, operative costs are financed from fees that are subject to differentiation, and provision is self-sustainable. Financial sustainability in this case is facilitated by one specific characteristic of the administrative organization in Bogota which is stratification[5]. Domiciliary public services operate under a cross-subsidy system, the so-called estratos. This system provides an important administrative function by which the upper classes pay higher rates for services or utilities, subsidizing the cost of services for the lower classes.

Half of the municipalities in metropolitan Lima have financial deficits due to low payment rates and collected fees that do not cover expenditures, and provision has to be financed by intergovernmental transfer.

In MCMA, unlike Bogota and Lima, there are no formal fares for this service. Instead, citizens tip drivers and waste pickers who collect, sort and transport waste. Other than labor costs, the operation is highly subsidized and is funded by local governments on a shared-costs basis. Financial capacity is weak in general, and there is great variation in between jurisdictions.

Official data show more than 90% service coverage in all three cities, yet these figures often exclude informal settlements. In Bogota, for instance, official coverage is informed by the stratification system, which omits informal housing. In Lima, the mean coverage figure, 90% (MINAM 2014), hides the important variation across municipalities. In MCMA coverage is usually based on Census registrations that are limited in including informal housing. As in other cases peripheries tend to receive lower coverage and quality. Similarly, in MCMA there are important spatial disparities, with lower coverage in the northeast periphery, and there are significant problems of frequency and quality in the service. Table B.1 in Appendix B summarizes the main findings on this service.

---

[5]This cross-subsidy system consists of six 'estratos' based on socio-economic criteria: Stratum 1 includes the lowest income population and stratum 6 the highest income population.

*5.2 Water delivery*

Providing an adequate water supply in metropolitan areas is technically and politically very complex. Market and state failures have resulted in intricate arrangements for service provision that involve four broad actors: public, informal, community-based, and private operators that participate as part of public-private partnerships (Jones et al. 2014). In MCMA the federal government is involved in water regulation through the National Water Commission (CONAGUA), which is in charge of authorizing the use of national water, the bulk supply of water, the construction and operation of the infrastructure, and the preservation of aquifers. There is the Federal Basin Agency for the Valley of Mexico (Aguas del Valle de Mexico) and the Water and Sewer Metropolitan Commission. Piped water services must be provided by local governments. Municipalities decide whether to manage and operate their water systems directly or through decentralized public bodies. In Mexico City proper, SACMEX is the decentralized body responsible for providing water to the sixteen boroughs. In addition, four private firms attend to some segments of the water service across the boroughs[6]. In the states of Mexico and Hidalgo, 48% of municipalities operate mixed provision schemes where the state, the municipality and neighborhood committees overlap; 28% of municipalities have their own decentralized company; 10% of municipalities have water services operated by community/neighborhood bodies; and 14% of municipalities are direct producers. Informal mechanisms, the resale of water and clandestine connections are the only sources of water available to residents in several areas of the city (Rosales 2015).

In Metropolitan Lima, water is provided by Potable Water and Sewerage Service of Lima (SEDAPAL), a public company operating under a private legal regime. SEDA-PAL depends on the National Ministry of Housing and is regulated by the National Superintendence of Sanitation Services (SUNASS), a public decentralized organization. SUNASS, in turn, regulates and supervises water and sanitation provision and pricing. The National Authority of Water (ANA) administers and monitors natural sources of water and authorizes the volumes of water that service providers can take. According to Law 28696, SEDAPAL provides water and sanitation services to Lima and Callao provinces. Other areas can be included through a housing-sector Ministerial Resolution if there is territorial continuity and the service can be technically provided by SEDAPAL.

Bogota's Water Enterprise (Aguas de Bogota) provides services to Bogota and eleven nearby towns. The company operates at a regional level as a private corporation. Aguas de Bogota is subject to Law 142 and to all other norms that modify this law. The company is regulated by the Commission for the Regulation of Drinking Water and Basic Sanitation (CRA), which also sets the fares. Aguas de Bogota is the subsidiary company of a public enterprise, Acueducto, which provides water and sewerage services. Acueducto's service model in Bogota is based on division of the metropolitan area into five zones. Acueducto provides the service to the whole metropolitan area, not as a public but as a private firm.

Even though the Constitution allows voluntary cooperation, the supply of water services in MCMA lacks intergovernmental, horizontal and institutional coordination. Asymmetries in provision are significant because small municipalities are unable to benefit from economies of scale or to internalize positive spillover effects. The provision of water is a municipal function in Bogota, but the same company delivers the service to the whole metropolitan area. This provision, however, is determined by the private legal status of the producer rather than by formal horizontal coordination between Soacha and Bogota DC. Likewise, in metropolitan Lima, horizontal coordination lacks relevance because SEDAPAL is a central entity that supplies the whole metropolitan area (see Table B.2 in the appendix).

In MCMA as a whole, tariffs cover only 64% of operating costs and the rest of the cost has to be subsidized by the government. Only in Mexico City proper are subsidies based on geographic location and depend on the socioeconomic characteristics of each

---

[6]Mexico City is divided into four zones receiving commercial and maintenance services. Zone A includes three boroughs in the northwest and is served by SAPSA. Zone B comprises four boroughs and is served by Industrias del Agua de la Ciudad de México. Zone C incorporates four boroughs which are serviced by Tecnología y Servicios del Agua. Zone D covers five boroughs and is provided by Agua de México.

neighborhood. Payment rates are sufficient to maintain some financial stability. In contrast, municipalities in the State of Mexico show significant heterogeneity depending on the provision scheme and the capacity to collect tariffs. Small jurisdictions that do not meet the requirements for establishing their own operator are the worst-off financially because they lack access to specific public resources. As with other services, tariffs in Bogota are determined according to the cross-subsidy system. Operational costs are covered by fares and the company is considered financially healthy. The situation in Lima is similar, with the operation financed by collected tariffs. There are some consumption subsidies, and a transition to socioeconomic stratification is under way.

Official coverage data focuses on formal provision. The available data shows 100% coverage in formal neighborhoods of Bogota DC and around 82% in Soacha. In Lima, coverage is approximately 89%, with running water provided 24 hours a day in central Lima and between 19 and 22 hours a day in the rest of the metropolitan area. The quality of the service and the water itself accomplish minimum standards. In MCMA 79% of the population live in houses with a piped water connection; however only 72% of the population has daily access to water. In this metropolitan area daily access to water is highly unevenly spatially distributed and most peripheral municipalities and boroughs have extremely low availability. In these peripheries not only the service, but also the water itself is poor quality. The service is severely affected by aging and poorly-maintained pipes which can result in the loss of more than 25% of the water.

### 5.3 Public transport

In MCMA, public transportation is provided under varied government and concessional supply schemes. Public transport consists of the following systems: subway (Metro), rapid transit bus (Metrobus and Mexibus), light train, trolleybus, the Passenger Transport Network (RTP), a suburban train (Suburbano), Eco-bici (a public bicycle-sharing system), and private bus concessions (colectivos). According to the latest origin-destination survey (INEGI 2007), approximately 50% of the 22 million daily journeys in the metropolis are covered by buses and microbuses (as transport concessions), but Bus Rapid Transit (BRT) systems that combine public and private participation, have experienced the largest expansion in recent years. Some of these systems – subway, light train, trolleybus, the RTP and Eco-bici – operate only or mostly in Mexico City proper. The governance of public transport involves the following stakeholders: federal, state and local transport authorities, private transport companies and, at least on paper, a transportation metropolitan commission. In addition, there is a large informal sector. Despite the local nature of the service, public transport is generally provided by intermediate level governments (Fernández 2002). Intermediate level governments operating the public transport is the prevailing situation in Mexican municipalities which, despite holding institutional powers that allow them to intervene in the formulation and implementation of public passenger transport programs, have delegated the task to state governments due to their lack of the human, technical and financial resources needed to fully assume regulation and service management (IMCO 2012). In Mexico City proper the local Ministry of Mobility is in charge of planning and managing public transport. In the municipalities of the State of Mexico, planning and regulation of public transport concessions is the responsibility of the Ministry of Mobility, while the Ministry of Communications runs the mass-transit system, Mexibus. In the state of Hidalgo regulation and planning is based on the Transport Law and undertaken by a decentralized agency dependent on the Ministry of the interior (OECD 2015). Some municipalities have a transport and transit agency that is responsible for regulating local traffic and the building and maintenance of roads. The Metropolitan Commission (COMETRAVI) was created in 1994 through an agreement signed by the Federal Ministry of Transport and Communications and the governments of the State of Mexico and Mexico City proper. However, COMETRAVI is a non-operating agency.

In Bogota, the BRT Transmilenio and local buses form the core of public transport services and cover over 50% of journeys taken, with walking and motorcycles as significant modes of transport in the peripheries. The Ministry of Transportation is in charge of formulating and adopting policies, plans, programs and projects at the national level. The Ministry of Mobility operates at the municipal level in Bogota and Soacha. These two local ministries are advised to work in coordination to solve mobility and transport problems. The rest of the municipalities do not have such local ministries.

In Lima, provincial municipalities are in charge of regulating public transportation, but in the 1990's Peru adopted a public transportation model with little regulation and dominated by private supply. Since 2010 a BRT line, COSAC, has connected the north and the south of the city. A group of private companies run the COSAC service by means of a concession. In 2012 the first metro line was inaugurated to connect the east with the south, and a second line is under construction. The operation of metro lines is also given as a concession to private companies. These two systems represent only 4.4% and 3.4% of journeys in the metropolis respectively (Survey, Lima Como Vamos, 2015). Most metropolitan trips are taken on private bus lines that obtain authorization for specific routes from the municipalities of Lima and Callao and "rent" these authorizations to bus owners and drivers. This system is known as the commission-affiliation system. Since the companies receive a payment per vehicle operating and not per passenger, there is an excess of vehicles competing for passengers. There are 561 authorized routes with 38,000 vehicles in Lima and Callao (Ministerio de Transportes y Comunicaciones 2016).

The different public transport alternatives in MCMA do not operate as an integrated system. There is significant institutional and vertical as well as horizontal fragmentation. Efforts to better integrate or coordinate transportation systems are limited to the integration of the subway, Metrobus and Ecobici payment systems, but these only cover Mexico City proper. In the State of Mexico there is a predominance of 'colectivos'. A suburban train has operated between downtown Mexico City and some of the municipalities since 2008. The project was formulated and implemented mainly by the federal government, with some State of Mexico and Mexico City government involvement.

In metropolitan Lima, an agreement was reached to allow Callao and Lima to grant permits to private companies to operate across both provinces. However, lack of provincial coordination has resulted in overlapping routes. Institutional coordination is also problematic, and there are three different payment systems in the city. Metro and Metropolitano do not operate in Callao.

In Bogota, the 2016–2020 Development Plan seeks to strengthen an integrated system of public transportation including the collective public transportation and individual public transportation services (Bogota 2015). The program is also pursuing improvements to regional connectivity by inter-jurisdictional cooperation. However, the initiative has remained limited, and for instance Transmilenio has only four stations in Soacha. There is a consolidated model of infrastructure development, but this model is controlled by the central government.

In the MCMA, the financial sustainability of government-operated transport systems is precarious. They are heavily subsidized and their cost-revenue structures are not subject to technical analysis, leading to significant inefficiency. Excessive subsidization has contributed to local governments' financial burden. 'Colectivos' face financial constraints for investment, maintenance and operation. The system with the highest prices and in the best financial situation is the suburban train, but it requires significant funding for investment and maintenance. Bogota's BRT system has been sustainable due to resources injected by the district government, otherwise the tariffs would be insufficient to keep it running. The intermunicipal buses are self-sustainable in the sense that they operate on their own revenue. And in Lima, the Metropolitano system operates at costs while the subway is subsidized by central government. The rest of the services are private and self-sustained.

In MCMA official public transport coverage is above 90%, but peripheral areas exhibit deficits which are often compensated for by informal supply. The same applies in Bogota and Lima, whose official statistics do not reveal significant disparities. According to interviewees' perceptions, substantial inefficiencies, poor quality, low capacity, poor safety, low frequency and high prices are critical problems that require attention in all three of the metropolises.

Overall, services in MCMA are the most fragmented and have the lowest performance in terms of efficiency and equity. Public transportation is the service with the weakest governance and poorest performance in the three metropolises.

Table 1: Classification of service provision schemes

|  | MA Bogota | MA Lima | MA Mexico City |
| --- | --- | --- | --- |
| Piped water | In consolidation | Consolidated | Fragmented |
| Waste recollection | In consolidation | In consolidation | Fragmented |
| Public transport | In consolidation | Fragmented | Fragmented |

*Source*: Authors' elaboration

### 5.4 The models of service provision

Despite the established structures of government, intergovernmental relations and decentralization processes, metropolitan governance structures differ not only across metropolises, but also across sectors within the same metropolis. Arrangements for service provision and production and the related legal structures and rules vary depending on the local context and the service to be provided. The multiple forms of organization for the provision of services illustrate the diversity of governance structures and their evolution. We use the concept of consolidation to classify different governance schemes. Consolidation is understood here as a condition in which the supply area of a service is metropolis-wide. Metropolis-wide supply areas can be achieved by means of production arrangements or by annexation. Metropolitan governance can be classified into three categories: i) fragmented, where provision and production organization preserve the administrative structure of the metropolitan area, and there are no coordination arrangements or other formal or informal efforts to deliver metropolitan wide services; ii) consolidated, where a service is provided and produced completely or mostly by one entity; and iii) in consolidation, where different schemes, public or private, formal or informal, are aimed to build a metropolitan approach for service supply, with metropolitan zones gradually incorporated into the service supply area. See Table 1 for a summary.

The three services in the Metropolitan area of Bogota are classified as in consolidation. Transmilenio provides public transportation services in part of Soacha, and the Water Enterprise of Bogota also increasingly provides services outside the capital district. The consolidation of metropolitan area-wide service supply is explained to a good extent by the fact that the main political jurisdiction contains more than 80% of the population and covers most of the urban area. Actually, the metropolitan area as such has been in consolidation due to the historic process of annexation of surrounding municipalities. New areas beyond Bogota DC have been incorporated into the capital district and to the service delivery area over time. However, Soacha remains outside Bogota DC even though it is a rapidly-growing territory in demographic terms and has strong functional relations with Bogota.

In Lima, the water service is consolidated because the public company SEDAPAL provides water to the whole metropolitan area. Waste collection services are in consolidation with intermunicipal agreements seeking to coordinate and cooperate to deliver the service by means of associations of municipalities. However, so far, such initiatives have made slow progress. The transport service is fragmented. However, in the near future proposals may arise, since the subway service is expected to cover the province of Callao.

In Mexico City, piped water, waste collection and public transportation services are fragmented because they are mainly provided by multiple local governments and organizations with almost a complete lack of arrangements for metropolitan cooperation and coordination.

We find that the three models have implications for coordination, financial sustainability and coverage. Inter-jurisdictional coordination and cooperation and central government schemes are not observed in fragmented services. Services in consolidation relate to diverse arrangements for integrating or expanding the service area. Consolidation has depended mostly on national government initiatives and structures, although some form of cooperation or coordination may be necessary at lower levels. Fragmentation entails greater financial difficulties, especially when small governments and municipalities with low financial and fiscal capacity are unable to achieve economies of scale or their administrative structures lack the necessary resources. The more consolidated a service governance structure is, the better its financial capacities appear to be. Generally, the greatest difficulties in all cities and sectors are related to expenditure on infrastructure and investment. Consolidation contributes to better coverage and quality, and also to more equal access to services.

## 6    Final Remarks

This study has responded to the relative gap in understanding the specific empirical experiences of metropolitan governance of the delivery of public services in Latin America. Given that jurisdictional fragmentation is an inherent characteristic of metropolitan areas, distinguishing between provision and production/supply has helped us to identify variations across services and cities. In this comparative analysis of metropolitan governance in Mexico City, Bogota and Lima we have found not only that governance structures differ, but also that in some instances service supply is adapted to accommodate specific needs and sociopolitical contexts, even if such arrangements do not necessarily correspond to local rationalities. Such is the case of water provision in Lima, where the service is supplied by a public company that depends on the national government. In the metropolitan area of Bogota, institutional arrangements have been modified to gradually expand the supply of transport services to areas beyond the capital district as far as the municipality of Soacha. Although this has been a slow and problematic process, Transmilenio has established a few stations in Soacha. Another example is the water company in Bogota, which supplies the capital district as a public service and supplies other municipalities as a private company via arrangements with local governments. Also in Lima, some effort has been made towards intermunicipal coordination in the waste-management sector by means of associations of municipalities.

Even though the water service in Lima is the most consolidated governance structure discussed here, water services are provided by an agency which depends on the national government. Locally-guided projects or initiatives are weaker. Secondly, the consolidation processes in Bogota are strongly related to the historic annexation of territories to the main city. Third, the relatively good financial performance in service provision in Bogota is due to the cross-subsidy system. Fourth, despite the absence of metropolitan governments, governance can solve problems. The quality of that governance in turn affects technical, financial and social outcomes and performance. These cases exemplify how service supply with a metropolitan approach is not necessarily a process in which fragmented areas are governed by a single entity that provides all services to the wider territory, but can be a slow process of consolidation led by various arrangements and actors across sectors and jurisdictions.

On the other hand, the metropolitan area of Mexico City is a case in which coordination, financial sustainability and equity in every public service is strongly affected by high fragmentation which overpowers any approach to interjurisdictional coordination and cooperation for economic and social efficiency. Despite constitutional autonomy for voluntary intermunicipal cooperation, there are very few instances of coordination. It is not possible to conclude, however, that the lack of coordination and poor governance derive purely from the administrative fragmentation of the territory. In this specific metropolitan area, political economic factors appear to play a determining role in explaining the weak metropolitan governance structures including party and political competition between states and between municipalities; three-year municipal government terms; a culture of all-embracing political power and others.

We argue that fragmentation creates substantial difficulties in providing urban services. Yet empirically, governance for service provision is place-specific and depends on local political culture and overarching state legal frameworks. In the absence of formal metropolitan government, the operating structures of governance can reverse the negative impact of fragmentation. Lastly, metropolitan structures can vary to accommodate the characteristics of the services provided.

While these findings are not generalizable, they illustrate the significant empirical variation to be found across metropolises and sectors. They also illustrate the need, in less developed countries, for a debate on metropolitan governance that goes beyond the traditional approach to jurisdictional fragmentation and metropolitan governments. These findings can be used as a basis from which to identify questions for future comparative research or further in-depth case studies either by sector or by metropolitan area. Future work in our research will include in-depth analysis by sector to deal with questions that include the historical evolution of metropolitan configurations; the way politics have shaped metropolitan bureaucracy and government; how civil participation and transparency are embedded in metropolitan governance organization; and private actors' role in the production of services.

## Acknowledgement

We gratefully acknowledge the financial support and generosity of Brown International Advanced Research Institutes (BIARI), without which this research could not have been completed. We thank 2 anonymous reviewers for their comments on an earlier version of the manuscript and Professor Patrick Heller for his comments on our project. We would also like to show our gratitude to El Colegio de Mexico, and the Chamber of Commerce of Bogota for supporting the organization of different activities during the fieldwork in Mexico and Colombia. Finally, we wish to thank various people and organizations that participated in the workshops and interviews.

## References

Bahl R (2013) The decentralization of governance in metropolitan areas. In: Bahl R, Linn J, Wetzel D (eds), *Financing metropolitan governments in developing countries.* Cambridge, MA, Lincoln Institute of Land Policy, 85–106

Bird R, Slack E (2007) An approach to metropolitan governance and finance. *Environment and Planning C: Government and Policy* 25[5]: 729–755. CrossRef.

Boex J, Lane B, Yao G (2013) An assessment of urban of urban public service delivery in South Asia: An analysis of institutional and fiscal constraints. Urban Institute Center on International Development and Governance Research Report. Washington, D.C. The Urban Institute

Bogota (2015) Proyecto plan de desarrollo 2016-2020. Available in: http://www.sdp.gov.-co/sites/default/files/20160429_proyecto_pdd.pdf

Cenizal C (2015) Governing the metropolis: The evolution of cooperative metropolitan governance in Mexico City's public transportation. Master dissertation. Massachusetts Institute of Technology, Cambridge MA, USA

Ciudad Limpia (2017) Tarifas aplicadas para los usuarios no aforados. Available in: http://www.ciudadlimpia.com.co/site/index.php?.option=com_content&view=article&id=17&Itemid=159

DANE (2017) Boletín técnico. Available in: https://www.dane.gov.co/files/investigaciones/-boletines/transporte/bol_transp_IVtrim16.pdf

Diálogos de Políticas Pública (2015) Nota de política pública de descentralización

Durand M (2012) Waste management in a developing city: Capitalising on current difficulties in Lima? *Flux* 87[1]: 18–28

Feiock R (2004) Introduction: Regionalism and institutional collective action. In: Feiock R (ed), *Metropolitan Governance: Conflict, Competition, and Cooperation.* Georgetown University Press, Washington, DC, 3–16

Fernández J (2002) Servicios públicos municipales. Instituto Nacional de Administración Pública (INAP), México

IMCO (2012) Propuestas transversales. Acciones urgentes para las ciudades del futuro. Instituto Mexicano para la Competitividad, México

INEGI (2007) Encuesta origen-destino 2007. Instituto Nacional de Estadística y Geografía, México

INEI (2014) Una mirada a lima metropolitana. https://www.inei.gob.pe/media/MenuRecursivo/publicaciones_digitales/Est/Lib1168/libro.pdf

Jones H, Clench B, Harris D (2014) The governance of urban service delivery in developing countries. Report overseas development institute. march, 2014. available in: https://www.odi.org/publications/8329-urban-services-poverty

Lowery D (2000) A transactions costs model of metropolitan governance: Allocation versus redistribution in Urban America. *Journal of Public Administration Research and Theory* 10[1]: 49–78. CrossRef.

Mayor of Bogota (2015) Somos un territorio metropolitano. Available in: http://www.sdp.gov.co/imagenes_portal/documentacion/OficPrensa/Cartilla_Somos_Un_Territorio_Metropolitano.pdf

MINAM (2014) Sexto informe nacional de residuos solidos de la gestion del ambito municipal y no municipal 2013. Ministerio del Ambiente, MINAM. Lima, Peru. http://redrrss.minam.gob.pe/material/20160328155703.pdf

Ministerio de Transportes y Comunicaciones (2016) Autoridad de transporte urbano para Lima y Callao: propuesta conceptual, Cooperación Alemana. https://www.mtc.gob.pe/estadisticas/Autoridad de Transporte Urbano para Lima y Callao-144dpi.pd

Oates W (1997) On the welfare gains from fiscal decentralization. *Journal of Public Finance and Public Choice* 2-3: 83–92

OECD (2015) Getting mobility in the Valle de México on the right track, in OECD territorial reviews: Valle de México, Mexico. Technical report, Paris. CrossRef.

Parks R, Oakerson R (1989) Metropolitan organization and governance: A local public economy approach. *Urban Affairs Quarterly* 25[1]: 18–29. CrossRef.

Parks R, Oakerson R (1993) Comparative metropolitan organization: Service production and governance structures in St. Louis (MO) and Allegheny County (PA). *Publius: The Journal of Federalism* 23[1]: 19–40

Perlman B, J. J, de D, Pineda G (2011) Rethinking a megalopolis: A metropolitan government proposal for the Mexico City metro area. *State and Local Government Review* 43[2]: 144–150

Prud'homme R (1995) The dangers of decentralization. *The World Bank Research Observer* 10[2]: 201–220

Rosales A (2015) Economía política del servicio de agua y saneamiento en la Ciudad de México. PhD thesis. CEDUA, El Colegio de México, México

SEDESOL, CONAPO, INEGI (2012) Delimitación de las Zonas Metropolitanas de México 2010. Secretaría de Desarrollo Social. Consejo Nacional de Población. Instituto Nacional de Estadística, Geografía e Informática

Slack E (2007) Managing the coordination of service delivery in metropolitan cities: The role of metropolitan governance. Policy research working papers. CrossRef.

Smith D (2014) World city populations 1950-2030. Available in: http://luminocity3d.org/WorldCity/#3/-7.36/-75.94

Storper M (2014) Governing the large metropolis. *Territory, Politics, Governance* 2[2]: 115–134. CrossRef.

Tiebout C (1956) A pure theory of local expenditures. *Journal of Political Economy* 64[5]: 416–424. CrossRef.

Treisman D (2000) Decentralization and the quality of government. Unpublished paper, University of California, Los Angeles. available in: https://www.imf.org/external/-pubs/ft/seminar/2000/fiscal/treisman.pdf

Trejo A (2013) Las Economías de las Zonas Metropolitanas de México en los Albores del Siglo XXI. Estudios Demográficos y Urbanos, 28(84), pp. 545-593. Distrito Federal. Centro de Estudios Demográficos, Urbanos y Ambientales. El Colegio de México

Yaro R, Ronderos N (2011) International metropolitan governance: Typology, case studies and recommendations. Developed for the Colombia urbanization review. The World Bank Group, Regional Plan Association

## A  Appendix: Fieldwork

*Guiding questions (focus groups and interviews)*

1. What is the role or what place does the service occupy in the metropolitan/urban agenda?

2. What is the general diagnosis (depending on the case) of the main problems faced by the provision of (water provision, waste recollection and public transport) at the metropolitan level and in the metropolitan periphery in particular?

3. In terms of coverage, to what extent can we speak of an accessible and universal service?

4. What is the assessment of the frequency and quality of the service?

5. What is the appreciation of the characteristics and the physical support of the service?

6. Are there infrastructural or operational deficiencies?

7. To what extent do authorities worry about improving the provision of the service?

8. What are the perspectives, limits and opportunities for the expansion of the service to reach metropolitan coverage?

9. What are the possibilities for an Integrated Metropolitan Service System?

10. What are the challenges for local governments in providing te service?

11. What are the general characteristics of the tariff system and the cost of provision?

12. What is the general evaluation of the financial sustainability in the provision of the service?

13. What is the evaluation of the current institutional and operational coordination between different jurisdictions and levels of government?

14. What efforts are developing at different tiers of government to improve the service?

15. What is the role of political factors in the operation and provision of the service?

*Technical visits*

Ecatepec (Mexico City)
Melchor Ocampo (Mexico City)
Puente Piedra (Lima)
Soacha (Bogota)
Ciudad Bolivar (Bogota)

*Interviews*

1. Bogota

Municipality of Soacha (director of public services)
Community leader (Ciudad Bolivar)

Table A.1: Focus groups: schedule and participants

| City | Actors | Water | Waste | Transport |
|---|---|---|---|---|
| Bogota | Academia | — | — | — |
| | Civil society | Recicle Colombia (NGO) | TECHO (ONG) | — |
| | Local government | Local secretary of the environment | Local secretary of the environment | Transmilenio |
| | Provider | Empresa de Agua de Bogotá-"Acueducto" | Empresa de Agua de Bogotá-"Acueducto" | Transmilenio |
| Lima | Academia | — | — | — |
| | Civil society | Ciudad Nuestra, Lima Como vamos, Contribuyentes por respeto (NGOs) | Alternativa, AFIN (NGOs) | Luz Ambar, Transitemos (NGOs) |
| | Local government | | Waste management office (municipalities of Lima, Miraflores, San Miguel and Puente Piedra) | Urban development office (Ate) |
| | Provider | | Waste management office (municipalities of Lima, Miraflores, San Miguel and Puente Piedra) | |
| Mexico city | Academia | Expert on metropolitan water governance (Centro Interdisciplinario de Estudios Metropolitanos) | Expert on solid waste managment (Universidad Nacional Autonoma de Mexico) | Expert on urban transportation and mobility (El Colegio de Mexico) |
| | Civil society | Isla Urbana (NGO) | Agencia de Gestión Urbana-AGU (Urban Management Agency) | Institute for Transportation and Development Policy (ITDP) and ASIICSO Habitus (NGO) |
| | Local government | Local secretary of the environment | Local secretary of the environment | — |
| | Provider | Sistemas de Agua de la Ciudad de Mexico-SACMEX | Local authorities of street cleaning (Servicio de limpia, Cuauhtemoc) | Passenger Transport Network System (RTP) |

2. Lima

Municipality of Puente Piedra (manager of urban development)
Autoridad Autónoma del Sistema Eléctrico de Transporte Masivo de Lima y Callao –
AATE (agengy in charge of the Metro Project in Lima and Callao)
Transport office, Municipalidad de Lima
SEDAPAL (public company of water and sanitation)


3. Mexico City Metropolitan Area

Ecatepec (They had accepted the meeting, but refuse to answer the questions)
Melchor Ocampo Municipality (Mayor)
Melchor Ocampo (director of urban services)
Melchor Ocampo (director of water provision)
Melchor Ocampo (coordinator or public transport)
Consultant of Ferrocarriles Suburbanos (Suburban train)




## B   Appendix: Summary of findings

Table B.1: Aspects of metropolitan governance in the waste collection service

| | | | Bogota | Lima | Mexico City |
|---|---|---|---|---|---|
| PROCESS | | Coordination | * There is no coordination for the provision of the service. Each municipal entity chooses a public or private operation.<br>* Before the absence of horizontal coordination, small municipalities sometimes allowed the Cundinamarca department company to provide the service.<br>* There is some institutional coordination, mainly with the Association of Bogota Recyclers. | * The Metropolitan System of Treatment and Elimination of Solid Waste does not include Callao.<br>* Despite strong normative incentives for coordination and cooperation, there are no adequate mechanisms to ensure institutional coordination.<br>* Advancement in horizontal coordination through mancomunities. | * There is some institutional coordination within the Federal District.<br>* In municipalities of the State of Mexico some public-private coordination takes place when private companies provide the service as concessions.<br>* An environmental metropolitan commission focuses mainly on air pollution problems.<br>* There is no metropolitan institutional action and an absence of horizontal coordination among jurisdictions. |
| RESULTS | Supply | Financial Sustainability | * Fees are subject to the socioeconomic classification of properties (estratos). This creates the possibility of cross-subsidies.<br>* Fees vary from 3,096 to 28,508 Colombian pesos.<br>* Total fees include sweeping and cleaning,commercialization, collection and transport.<br>* Financially sustainable. | * Significant differences in payment rates across municipalities.<br>* Reliance on intergovernmental transfers to provide the service where there is a low payment rate.<br>* 17 districts have a 50% deficit in expenditure coverage.<br>* Generally not self-sustainable, but there are significant differences across districts. | * No official tariffs or fees.<br>* Payment is made via tips to drivers and waste pickers.<br>* Costs shared between waste management and other areas of municipal public services.<br>* Operation under a subsidy scheme.<br>* Variation across jurisdictions.<br>* Weak financial capacity and unsustainable provision. |
| | Demand | Access, coverage and quality | * Coverage of more than 90% in the majority of municipalities, both in Bogota and in the metropolitan area (official data collected only in formal settlements)<br>* Success in reaching all socioeconomically vulnerable areas via the stratification transfer system. | * Estimated 90% coverage<br>* Problems of low quality<br>* Variation across areas depending on socioeconomic conditions | * Covers between 88 and 98% of households<br>* Lower coverage in the Northeast periphery<br>* Highly inefficient in quality and frequency but with great variation across jurisdictions. |

Table B.2: Aspects of metropolitan governance in water provision

| | | | Bogota | Lima | Mexico City |
|---|---|---|---|---|---|
| PROCESS | | Coordination | * There is coordination between the municipalities. Even though water provision is a municipal function, the Bogotá company (EAAB) competes as a public society but with private logic. Provision to the area of Soacha next to Bogota. | * Intermunicipal coordination is not an issue since all municipalities are serviced by SEDAPAL.<br>* Weak vertical coordination between SEDAPAL and municipalities in Lima and Callao. | * A multiplicity of actors and jurisdictions translates into fragmented models of provision.<br>* Rare cases of municipal association; weak intermunicipal coordination.<br>* Weak vertical coordination with Federal institutions. |
| RESULTS | Supply | Financial sustainability | * Tariffs are fixed according to six levels of "estratos" defined by the socioeconomic status of households.<br>* $6m^3$ of water is provided to each household of estrato 1 for free.<br>* Operational costs are covered by tariffs.<br>* The company is considered financially healthy. | * Operational costs covered by tariffs.<br>* Infrastructure investments not covered by tariffs.<br>* Large infrastructure projects financed by central government transfers.<br>* Tariffs have subsidies based on consumption.<br>* SEDAPAL is transitioning to a subsidy based on socioeconomic status.<br>* Overall, SEDAPAL is a financially healthy company. | * Tariffs cover 64% of operating costs, government subsidizes the rest.<br>* Subsidies in Mexico City based on geographic criterion depending on the socioeconomic classification of neighborhood.<br>* There is significant heterogeneity in the financial situation among jurisdictions depending on the provision scheme.<br>* Provision in Mexico City appears to be relatively stable financially.<br>* Small municipalities in the State of Mexico that do not meet the criteria for establishing their own service operator have worse financial conditions. |
| | Demand | Access, coverage and quality | * Almost 100% in legalized neighborhoods.<br>* In Bogotá 98.6% of neighborhoods; in Soacha 82.8%; in Sabana 96.3%. | * Around 89% of households have a water connection inside their house.<br>* Availability of the service is not a problem.<br>* 24 hours of running water on average in Lima Centro.<br>* Between 19 and 22 hours in the periphery. | * Piped water connection inside the houses of approximately 79% of metropolitan population.<br>* 72% of population has daily access to water.<br>* Highly uneven spatial distribution of access to the daily water service.<br>* Most peripheral municipalities and boroughs have lower availability. |

Table B.3: Aspects of metropolitan governance in public transport

| | | | Bogota | Lima | Mexico City |
|---|---|---|---|---|---|
| PROCESS | | Coordination | * There is a consolidated model for the construction of infrastructure, but without a real metropolitan approach.<br>* Intermunicipal transportation is Departments' responsibility.<br>* Transmilenio offers a service to only four stations outside of Bogota's borders, in Soacha | * The system is fragmented, but there have been efforts to integrate it jurisdictionally.<br>* Integration with private operators is necessary.<br>* Lima and Callao have agreed that both can provide permission to private companies to operate in both provinces.<br>* There is no integration nor coordination between systems. For instance, different payment systems operate in the city for the Metro, the Metropolitano and secondary routes. | * Provision is fragmented 'administratively' between different transport systems and jurisdictionally between Mexico City and metropolitan municipalities.<br>* There have been projects towards the integration and coordination of systems but the initiative has not developed successfully, with the exception of some elements such as payment methods (Metro and Metrobus). |
| RESULTS | Supply | Financial Sustainability | * The system is sustainable due to financial support, but is not self-sustainable.<br>* Transmilenio is funded directly by the District Government of Bogotá.<br>* The SITP has problems with being financially sustainable based on fares taken.<br>* In the rest of the municipalities, intermunicipal metropolitan buses are run privately, and most are financially sustainable. | * After almost six years the Metropolitano has reached equilibrium point where the outgoings of the operation are covered by customer fares.<br>* The Metro is subsidized by central government which allows people to access the service; otherwise fares would increase and become unaffordable for some population groups. | * Transport systems operating only in Mexico City are heavily subsidized.<br>* Lack of technical analysis of costs and income structures.<br>* Variability between systems and jurisdictions.<br>* The commuter train, Suburbano, represents a case of uncertain financial sustainability.<br>* Consession services face important financial investment, maintenance and operation problems. |
| | Demand | Access, coverage and quality | * Good coverage in general.<br>* Problems in terms of quality in municipalities outside the city of Bogotá. | * High coverage but low quality.<br>* 54% of Limeños think that transportation is one of the main problems in the city. Satisfaction with public transport is very low across the city | * Coverage is high in general, but peripheral areas experience problems with frequency or even lack formal transport services.<br>* Concession service is highly inefficient, with poor quality, poor safety and low environmental sustainability.<br>* The BRT system, Metrobus, and the Metro operate beyond capacity, affecting quality.<br>* The suburban train is best rated in terms of frequency, safety and quality, but is also the most expensive. |

**REGION**

The Journal of ERSA
Powered by WU

Volume 5, Number 3, 2018, 97–109
DOI: 10.18335/region.v5i3.223

journal homepage: region.ersa.org

# Market Access and the Concentration of Economic Activity in a System of Declining Cities

**Luis Eduardo Quintero[1], Paula Restrepo[2]**

[1] Johns Hopkins University, Baltimore, MD, USA
[2] The World Bank, Washington, DC, USA

Received: 2 November 2017/Accepted: 16 October 2018

**Abstract.** While the positive effect of market access (MA) on population and economic growth has shown to be robust, the results in the literature were obtained in a context of population growth. This article examines the impact that MA has on a system of cities that has suffered a negative population shock. An extended version of the Brezis, Krugman (1997) model of life cycle of cities predicts that a system of cities experiencing population loss will see a relative reorganization of its population from small to larger cities, increasing population concentration. Accordingly, cities with higher MA will lose relatively more. We confirm these predictions using multiple definitions of MA with a comprehensive sample of cities in Eastern Europe and Central Asia, a region with declining population growth since 1990.

**Key words:** Market access, urban decline, demographic transition, Eastern Europe and Central Asia

## 1 Introduction: Market Access in a Declining System of Cities

Agglomeration economies quantify the impact on firms and worker's incomes of being located in larger and denser local markets (Combes, Gobillon 2015). Since firms trade with distant markets, these agglomeration economies can have spillovers. The trade literature has documented that the strength of these spillovers between countries can be determined positively by the size of the economies and negatively by its trading costs, usually measured with distance (Head, Mayer 2004), following gravity models (Anderson 1979).

The spillovers of agglomeration economies can be measured by market access (MA), a measure that is similar to market potential, but that leaves the focus economy size out to capture the partial effect of proximity to other markets. Empirical work often follows Harris (1954) and defines trade costs as being proportional to the inverse of distance. Using a notation similar to Henderson, Wang (2007), we define city MA:

$$MA_i(t) = \sum_{k \in j | j \neq i}^{N_{jt}-1} \frac{n_k(t)}{d_{ik}} \tag{1}$$

where $n$ is a measure of market size[1], $d_{ik}$ is the distance between city $i$ and $k$, and $N_{jt}$ is the total number of cities at time $t$[2].

Higher MA is expected to benefit the city's economy through higher average effective demand and average lower transportation costs for its exports to other cities. This increased demand applies to tradeable goods, but in equilibrium can affect local labor and non-tradeables. The positive effect of MA on economic output and population growth has been predominant in empirical results. Head, Mayer (2006), Bosker et al. (2010), and Combes et al. (2010) find that MA significantly increases local regional wages in different European regions. Fallah et al. (2010) find similar results for the US. These patterns have been less studied for developing economies but there are some robust results, such as Au, Henderson (2006) for China, Amiti, Cameron (2007) for Indonesia, and Quintero, Roberts (2018) for Latin America. To our knowledge, only one study has previously found a negative effect of MA (Duranton 2016).

The previous results focus on the impact of MA on productivity measured through wages. This is closely related to our analysis, but we focus instead on the effect on population growth, which is affected by differences in productivity too (Harris, Todaro 1970). Henderson, Wang (2007) and Redding, Sturm (2008) test the effect of MA precisely on population growth and find again a positive effect. Combes, Gobillon (2015) summarize estimates of MA impact and conclude that the positive effect of the economic size of distant locations and the spatial decay of this effect are rarely rejected empirically. These results have been obtained in a context of population growth. To test what would happen in the context of population decline, we perform our analysis in Eastern Europe and Central Asia, a region that has suffered a dramatic population decline in the last decades.

In contrast to most literature, we find a negative effect of MA. In a system of declining (population) cities, having a higher MA is found to be detrimental to population growth relative to the national trend. This result is robust to MA measures that use population. Alternative measures that use NLs are tested, and the results are weaker. These findings are in line with the theoretical predictions in Quintero, Restrepo (2017), which use the model found in Brezis, Krugman (1997) to simulate city population growth under the effects of a negative population shock and predict a relative reorganization of the urban population from small to larger cities. These findings highlight the importance of the insight in Glaeser, Gyourko (2005), which suggests population decline should be studied specifically and not assumed as a mirror image of positive growth.

A possible explanation for the negative impacts of MA in a declining system of cities is the effect it has on relative real income in the short run. The main prediction in Quintero, Restrepo (2017) is that a decline in population will have two main effects. First, differences in nominal wages across cities will be slow to adjust because productivity depends on historical cumulative production. Second, local costs, especially housing, will adjust downwards, creating a wedge between productivity and costs that were formerly balanced by the spatial equilibrium. This creates incentives for labor to reallocate from smaller to larger (formerly more productive) cities. In this context, MA can act as a push factor (an incentive to move out to get better pay elsewhere), as opposed to the traditional interpretation as a pull factor (an incentive to produce in a place that has access to larger markets to sell its local products).

## 2   Eastern Europe and Central Asia: A system of cities with declining population and increasing concentration

Eastern Europe and Central Asia (ECA)[3] has gone through a drastic population decline. 65% of the cities lost population between 1989 and 2010, with an average loss of 21%

---

[1]These markets are sometimes measured by local GDP. We use population to measure market size, and night lights (NLs) as a proxy in a robustness test.

[2]Fujita et al. (1999) emphasize that under imperfect competition, Harris' specification would need to include local prices. We lack this data and thus use the specification in equation (1), which is common. This is a differenced and linearized version of Au, Henderson (2006).

[3]ECA is Easter Europe and Central Asia as classified by the World Bank. The countries included are: Albania, Armenia, Azerbaijan, Belarus, Bosnia and Herzegovina, Bulgaria, Georgia, Kazakhstan, Kosovo, Kyrgyz Republic, Macedonia, Moldova, Montenegro, Romania, Russian Federation, Serbia, Tajikistan, Turkey, Turkmenistan, Ukraine, and Uzbekistan.

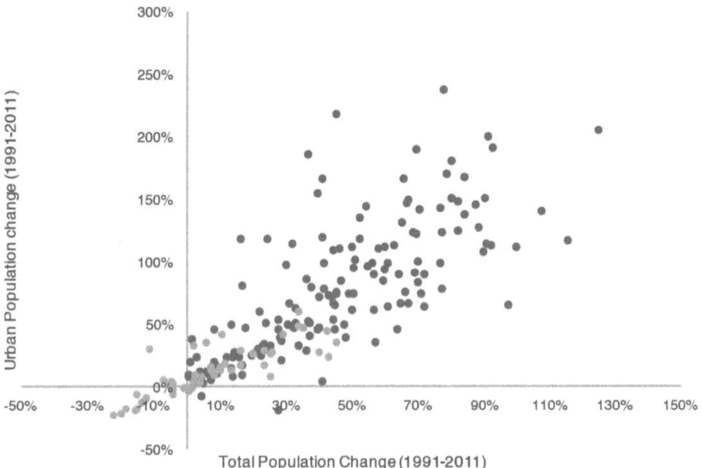



*Source*: UN World Population Prospects

Figure 1: Urban and total population growth, ECA (green) countries versus rest

for declining cities[4]. Table 1 gives an overview of the urban systems we use in our analysis. 11 out of 15 countries present negative population growth in at least one of the decades analyzed, while the others present low positive population growth. All present a decline in growth trends observed before 1989 (see footnote 5). Decline happens all across the city size distribution, as can be seen by comparing declining cities in different size subsamples. Furthermore, the decline is happening in cities that hold an important share of the national population. Figure 1 illustrates the extent of urban population decline of countries in the ECA region compared to others in the world. In particular, this is partially explained by declining fertility rates (Table 2) that have not been offset by immigration (Figure 2).

This structural change in the population trends began at a crucial moment in the history of the region, between 1989 and 1990, when the countries in the region that had command and control economies transitioned into market economies either because of the separation of the USSR or as part of independent reform movements (the earliest transition is observed in December 1989 and the latest in March 1992). It is not surprising that many ECA cities would lose population as they transition to a market economy. Many were probably artificially large given the influences of a command economy on industry and population location prior to the transition. More freedom of movement after this transition implied actual population movement, as people left unproductive and sectoral concentrated cities, and focused on more diverse ones (Andrienko, Guriev 2004, Commander et al. 2011, Kofanov, Mikhailova 2015). Similar patterns have been studied for the rust belt in the US (Yoon 2017) and Germany (Redding, Sturm 2008).

We take this population decline as an exogenous departure point or shock in our empirical work[5]. Thus, we do not attempt to further explain this shock but measure how MA affected cities heterogenous reaction to this shock.

---

[4]In contrast, the counties covered by Glaeser, Gyourko (2005), which studies population decline in metropolitan areas in the US, only show 6.72% of the counties considered losing population, with an average loss of 9%.

[5]We expect this structural population shock to occur precisely around 1989 because of the large economic and political regional changes discussed above. To confirm, we regress time on country dummies and population levels for the period 1960-2017, allowing for a structural break in one year in slope and constant. Iteratively, all years are tested as transition periods. As expected, 1990 is confirmed to be the year in which all countries present a statistically significant structural change. One year before (1989) and one and two years after (1991, 1992) also reject this hypothesis for some countries, but not for all. We also calculate the tests for structural break found in Gendron-Carrier et al. (2017) and confirm 1990 as the year with a structural break.

Table 1: Summary statistics

| Country | Period | Total population change (annual) | Urban population change (annual) | % of population living in shrinking cities | % of cities losing population | | |
|---|---|---|---|---|---|---|---|
| | | | | | all | >30k | >100k |
| Albania | 1989-2001 | -0.2 | 1.08 | 14.12 | 27.42 | 10 | 0 |
| | 2001-2011 | -0.55 | 1.65 | 47.25 | 82.26 | 60 | 0 |
| Belarus | 1989-2001 | -0.16 | 0.47 | - | - | - | - |
| | 2001-2014 | -0.39 | 0.22 | 26.87 | 70.8 | 43.33 | 21.43 |
| Bulgaria | 1989-2001 | -0.87 | -0.47 | - | - | - | - |
| | 2001-2013 | -0.81 | -0.42 | 67.66 | 94.7 | 91.11 | 55.56 |
| Georgia | 1989-2002 | -0.67 | -1.06 | 96.45 | 94.44 | 87.5 | 100 |
| | 2002-2014 | 0.2 | 0.35 | 6.92 | 31.48 | 0 | 0 |
| Kazakhstan | 1989-1999 | -0.62 | -0.68 | 59.8 | 69.86 | 67.92 | 68.18 |
| | 1999-2015 | 0.85 | 0.54 | 5.8 | 21.92 | 13.21 | 0 |
| Kyrgyz Rep. | 1989-1999 | 1.25 | 0.52 | 25.76 | 75.61 | 68 | 75 |
| | 1999-2013 | 1.21 | 1.2 | 12.49 | 42.86 | 33.33 | 0 |
| Moldova | 1989-2000 | -0.04 | -0.17 | 74.97 | 55.77 | 80 | 100 |
| | 2000-2015 | -0.16 | -0.31 | 40.88 | 81.13 | 80 | 0 |
| Poland | 1989-2003 | 0.06 | 0.13 | - | - | - | - |
| | 2003-2011 | -0.04 | -0.21 | 64.06 | 52.94 | 68.21 | 82.05 |
| Romania | 1992-2002 | -0.51 | -0.71 | 95.52 | 93.57 | 95.45 | 100 |
| | 2002-2011 | -0.93 | -0.73 | 90.41 | 90.86 | 92.54 | 90 |
| Russia | 1989-2000 | -0.01 | 0.004 | 50.15 | 65.19 | 54.51 | 50.92 |
| | 2000-2010 | -0.27 | -0.23 | 42.15 | 73.61 | 63.04 | 48.17 |
| Serbia | 1991-2002 | -0.09 | 0.43 | 50.9 | 46.37 | 55 | 60 |
| | 2002-2011 | -0.36 | -0.03 | 50.94 | 71.91 | 51.28 | 11.11 |
| Tajikistan | 1989-2000 | 1.75 | 0.02 | - | - | - | - |
| | 2000-2014 | 2.05 | 2.03 | 2.38 | 5.26 | 7.69 | 0 |
| Turkey | 1989-2000 | 1.61 | 2.73 | - | - | - | - |
| | 2000-2012 | 1.31 | 2.19 | 7.77 | 59.23 | 12.77 | 4.17 |
| Ukraine | 1989-2001 | -0.43 | -0.34 | 83.29 | 80 | 79.41 | 73.33 |
| | 2001-2013 | -0.59 | -0.35 | 75.48 | 82.06 | 81.02 | 75.56 |
| Uzbekistan | 1990-2000 | 1.87 | 1.15 | 11.88 | 10.17 | 9.84 | 22.22 |
| | 2000-2014 | 1.56 | 1.33 | 5.85 | 11.86 | 8.2 | 11.11 |

Table 2: Fertility Rates

| sub-region | 1960-1989 | 1989-2000 | 2000-2014 |
|---|---|---|---|
| Belarus, Moldova, Ukraine, Russia | 2.25 | 1.61 | 1.36 |
| Central Europe, Baltic Countries | 2.16 | 1.54 | 1.39 |
| Central Asia | 5.12 | 3.41 | 2.74 |
| Eastern Europe, Central Asia | 2.40 | 1.72 | 1.65 |
| World | 4.26 | 2.95 | 2.54 |

*Source*: World Development Indicators

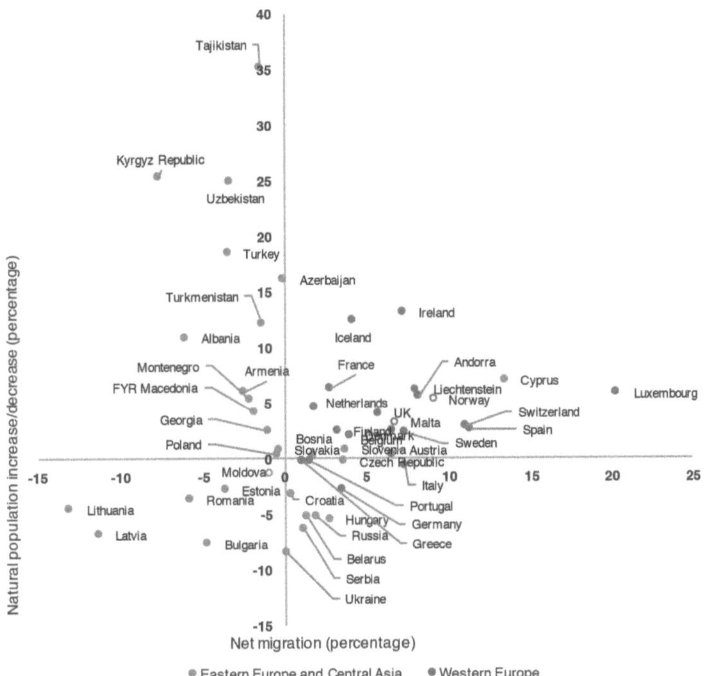


*Source*: UN World Population Prospects

Figure 2: Net migration and natural and total population growth, ECA (green) countries versus rest

## 3 Estimation of the Role of Market Access

Under this context declining population, we estimate the role of MA. We use the following estimating equation:

$$\Delta p_i = \beta_1 n_i + \beta_2 MA_i + \text{controls}_{i,c} \tag{2}$$

where $\Delta p_i$ is the annual percentage population change between years 2 and 3 (specified in Table 1), $n_i$ is the initial local market size, $MA_i$ is the MA defined in (1), variables are introduced in logarithms. We build controls for migration, fertility, and natural population growth rates, which vary by country $c$. We also control for secondary cities and groups of cities in agglomerations and include six location fundamental controls: (i) distance to border, (ii) distance to coast, (iii) forest coverage, (iv) annual precipitation, (v) average temperature in January and (vi) land usability.

Finally, to assuage any concern that the interpretation of our results which assumes a market economy for this region might be flawed, the population growth we use is calculated around 11 years after the transition, where population decline is still happening but the region's economic systems have probably fully transitioned. Figures B.1 and B.2 shows economic indices constructed to measure, to the extent that this is possible, integration to a market economy system. The indices indicate that, at the time of our analysis, the economic systems of the countries are at least as market oriented as those of other developing regions.

### 3.1 Identification

We are interested in the effect of MA in the relative loss of population of cities. MA can be endogenous to population change. For instance, natural features can provide advantages that affect population growth, and at the same time affect the probability of more towns locating closer together in nearby areas, increasing MA. The endogeneity is also suggested by Hausman tests. We use instrumental variables that affect population change only through their effect on MA: a measure of city centrality calculated as the

Table 3: Specifications of market access

| transportation costs, market size | population | NL |
| --- | --- | --- |
| geodetic distance | MA(g,pop) | MA(g,nl) |
| driving distance | MA(d,pop) | MA(d,nl) |

distance of each city to the center of the country; and a measurement of ranking of the city's size within its country. These instruments perform well in a first stage, and pass Sargan's test of overidentifying restrictions.

Our results stem from cross sectional variation: we analyze the impact of MA in the population growth of different cities exposed to the negative population shock, controlling for country effects and clustering errors at the country level. As such, unless we expect cities within the same country to adapt to a market economy at different speeds, we expect our results to be robust even in the context of different transition speeds between countries.

To further control for different cities being disproportionately affected by unobserved factors, like sectoral composition, in their transition to a market economy, we construct a dummy variable to identify places officially classified as a monotown (list obtained from Kuzmenko, Soldak 2010) in Soviet times for Russia (data only available for this country). We do not find a significant effect of this variable (these results available upon request).

### 3.2 Constructing Market Access Measures

We construct MA following equation (1) and restricting inclusion to cities in the same country. Table 3 shows the four versions of MA constructed: First, market size, $n_k(t)$, is measured using city population. Population is measured by each administrative unit (generally municipalities) obtained from official sources, for municipalities as small as 1,000. Despite having a shorter time frame than comparable datasets, our larger scope allows for conclusions to be applicable to the whole urban system population distribution[6].

Alternatively, we use NLs as a proxy of economic activity to capture market size. Henderson et al. (2011) discuss the benefits of using this data and present evidence of its validity as a proxy. NLs data provide a globally consistent data set that is comparable, across countries. Also, it is sampled uniformly (Henderson et al. 2012), and its measurement error is not related to development levels. Finally, NLs provide information about economic activity at levels of geographical disaggregation for which economic data is generally absent, which is the case of cities in ECA. We perform tests similar to those in Henderson et al. (2012) using subnational Gross Regional Domestic Product (GRDP) and find robust positive correlations that support the use of NLs (Table C.1).

There are two issues that affect the NL based measurements. First, the captured NL footprint, cannot be separated between municipalities whose NL emissions touch in space, forming agglomerations. We follow Roberts et al. (2015) to determine footprints and agglomerations[7] and use agglomerations as our observation level when dealing with municipalities in them. Since agglomerations are groupings of cities who work as a single functional entity, we expect any type of agglomeration benefits and spillovers to be shared as well. Second, the algorithm has a lower performance when identifying dimmer NLs in smaller places. As a consequence, some smaller cities included in the total sample are left out in the sample that has NLs available data (NLs sample). The average size of the city in the NLs sample is 100,670, compared to an average population of 64,470 in the total sample. The NLs sample is nearly half the size of the total sample.

Second, we use different measures of distance as a proxy of transportation costs for exports to other cities. Most literature uses geodetic distance calculated as distance

---

[6]As a contrast, Henderson, Wang (2007) build a data set on all metro areas over 100,000 from 1960 to 2000; the UN Statistics Division has a dataset since 1950, for cities only with more than 300,000 inhabitants.

[7]We identify a total of 352 agglomerations composed of a total of 2,358 cities.

between points on an oblate spheroid (Vincenty 1975), an approximation of the earth, ignoring any actual road system[8]. A more realistic measure, as suggested by Lall et al. (2004) and Combes, Gobillon (2015), is actual driving distances, which we construct using Open Source Routing Machine (OSRM) and OpenStreetMap[9].

## 4   Results and discussion

Table 4 shows the results of regressions of the model specified in equation 2. In the main specification that constructs MA using population, the estimated impact of MA is negative. A possible explanation for this effect is real income differences that result after a negative population shock and the effect these have in the influence of MA on population flows. The two main effects of a negative population shock discussed in Quintero, Restrepo (2017) are: First, frictions in the dynamics of productivity tend to maintain differences in nominal wages between large and small cities shortly after the shock, because productivity depends on the historical accumulation of production and knowledge. At the same time, housing prices decline in both cities due to the reduction in demand and the short run durable housing stock (Brueckner 2000). This changes the real incomes and creates incentives for labor to reallocate from smaller to larger cities (originally more productive but more expensive). The induced movement of population will be particularly strong for cities with larger MA because they have those larger, more productive, labor markets nearby for the fleeing population. Because of these income differences, and because smaller cities will have a relative higher MA[10] in a fixed system of cities, this result would also predict concentration of population in fewer larger cities after a negative population shock, which is consistent with the evidence[11].

The effect after instrumentation is only significant for the MA measures that use population, not our robustness test that uses NLs. One possible explanation comes from the interpretation of the channel through which MA impacts population growth. Our results suggest that the population flow is determined by being near populated places more than being near places with large economic activity. It could be the case that it is the access to large labor markets that matters the most, as opposed to just economic activity, which could be determined more by capital in cities focused on capital intensive or extractive industries.

Another possible interpretation of the difference in the results could come from the changes in the sample of cities used (see discussion in Section 3.2). The NLs sample of cities is smaller and concentrated in larger cities. If the negative effect of MA is mainly led by smaller cities, then our measurement of MA with NLs would not be appropriate, and we should rely on the population-based measurements. This result is in agreement with Greenstone et al. (2010), which discusses that the effect of MA is larger for smaller cities because they rely more on outside markets. Yet, results are robust to using either geodetic distance or driving distance, which makes the former preferable for this application given its much lower cost to calculate.

The role of local market size changes significantly when using measures with NLs and population. In specifications 1-4 a larger local market is associated with lower population loss, as predicted in the Brezis, Krugman (1997) model. The effect is not significant for the MA measure that uses NLs. As before, it could be the case that either local agglomeration economies are led by population size and not the magnitude of the economy, or that the effects are different because of sample selection implied by the nature of NL measurement. Finally, the effect of belonging to a formerly communist country is also different in the different specifications. Cities in former communist countries lost, on

---

[8]High altitudes imply errors in this approach. In the cities in our dataset, this does not seem to be an issue. Only Tajikistan and Kyrgyztan have few small towns with altitudes higher than 3.2 km, but their populations are lower than 5,000 (hence, very low weight in any MA calculation).

[9]Google maps data undergoes more strict validation but could not be used for the whole sample because of query volume restrictions. Calculation code is available from authors. Subsamples were tested in Google maps and no significant changes were found.

[10]In a system of $N$ cities, the largest city $j$ will only have access to smaller markets $-j$, while the other cities will have access to the large market $j$.

[11]See appendix section A

Table 4: The market access (MA) definitions follow notation in Table 3. The dependent variable is the annual population growth between year 2 and 3

| | MA(G,pop) | | MA(D,pop) | | MA(G,nl) | | MA(D,nl) | |
|---|---|---|---|---|---|---|---|---|
| | (1) | (2) | (3) | (4) | (5) | (6) | (7) | (8) |
| | OLS | IV | OLS | IV | OLS | IV | OLS | IV |
| *Market* | | | | | | | | |
| local mkt | 0.034* | 0.036* | 0.034* | 0.038* | 0.002 | -0.000 | 0.003 | 0.007 |
| | (13.41) | (12.97) | (13.40) | (12.42) | (0.63) | (-0.12) | (1.14) | (1.10) |
| mkt access | -0.002 | -0.072* | -0.001 | -0.071* | -0.013* | 0.006 | -0.011* | -0.022 |
| | (-0.62) | (-2.66) | (-0.37) | (-2.64) | (-2.57) | (0.31) | (-3.94) | (-1.17) |
| *Population Fundamentals* | | | | | | | | |
| nat. pop $\Delta$ | 0.007* | 0.005* | 0.007* | 0.005* | 0.009* | 0.010* | 0.010* | 0.009* |
| | (16.60) | (6.68) | (16.64) | (6.13) | (12.72) | (11.28) | (13.08) | (11.92) |
| net migration | 0.020* | 0.023* | 0.020* | 0.025* | 0.007* | 0.005 | 0.010* | 0.015+ |
| | (17.72) | (13.94) | (17.54) | (11.68) | (3.16) | (1.43) | (4.17) | (1.76) |
| Former | 0.142* | 0.097* | 0.143* | 0.101* | -0.055* | -0.045* | -0.063* | -0.075* |
| communist | (16.34) | (4.95) | (16.57) | (5.50) | (-3.20) | (-2.39) | (-3.66) | (-2.54) |
| Constant | -0.461 | 0.018 | -0.485 | -1.015 | 0.117 | 0.097+ | -0.050 | -0.200 |
| | (-10.26) | (0.09) | (-10.74) | (-4.90) | (2.25) | (1.72) | (-0.78) | (-0.76) |
| Observations | 5392 | 5381 | 5388 | 5377 | 2376 | 2368 | 2373 | 2365 |
| $R^2$ | 0.136 | 0.070 | 0.136 | 0.060 | 0.177 | 0.170 | 0.180 | 0.174 |
| Adjusted $R^2$ | 0.135 | 0.068 | 0.135 | 0.059 | 0.174 | 0.167 | 0.177 | 0.170 |

*Notes*: t statistics in parentheses; +: p < 0.10, *: p < 0.05

average, more population when considering the NLs sample, which could be again driven by sample selection. Other variables included have the expected values.

In conclusion, we present evidence suggesting that having higher MA – when operating in an environment of population decline – is detrimental to city population growth. The impact is negative for the MA measure that uses population as a proxy for market size, our preferred specification. We use a comprehensive sample of cities in Eastern Europe and Central Asia, which allows us to capture the effect on cities in all ranges of the city size distribution. Even in countries where all cities are losing population, this result suggests that cities with higher MA would lose relatively more. Our results contrast with the positive effects of MA found in the literature, which are estimated in a context of population growth. In times of population decline, nearby large markets could instead act as a push factor, as the remaining population see them as possible labor markets.

Future work should analyze the heterogeneity of the effects in cities of different sizes. Evaluating the causal impact of local market sizes in a context of decline is another interesting area to elaborate on the results of this letter.

## References

Amiti M, Cameron L (2007) Economic geography and wages. *The Review of Economics and Statistics* 89[1]: 15–29. CrossRef.

Anderson JE (1979) A theoretical foundation for the gravity equation. *The American Economic Review* 69[1]: 106–116

Andrienko Y, Guriev S (2004) Determinants of interregional mobility in Russia. *Economics of transition* 12[1]: 1–27. CrossRef.

Au CC, Henderson JV (2006) Are Chinese cities too small? *The Review of Economic Studies* 73[3]: 549–576. CrossRef.

Bosker M, Brakman S, Garretsen H, Schramm M (2010) Adding geography to the new economic geography: Bridging the gap between theory and empirics. *Journal of Economic Geography* 10[6]: 793–823. CrossRef.

Brezis ES, Krugman PR (1997) Technology and the life cycle of cities. *Journal of Economic Growth* 2[4]: 369–383. CrossRef.

Brueckner JK (2000) Urban growth models with durable housing: An overview. In: Huriot JM, Thisse J (eds), *Economics of Cities: Theoretical Perspectives*. Cambridge University Press, Cambridge, 263–289

Combes PP, Duranton G, Gobillon L, Roux S (2010) Estimating agglomeration economies with history, geology, and worker effects. In: Glaeser E (ed), *Agglomeration economics*. University of Chicago Press, Chicago IL. CrossRef.

Combes PP, Gobillon L (2015) The empirics of agglomeration economies. In: Duranton G, Henderson V, Strange W (eds), *Handbook of Regional and Urban Economics*, Volume 5. Elsevier, Oxford

Commander SJ, Nikoloski Z, Plekhanov A (2011) Employment concentration and resource allocation: One-company towns in Russia. European Bank for Reconstruction and Development

Duranton G (2016) Agglomeration effects in Colombia. *Journal of Regional Science* 56[2]: 210–238. CrossRef.

Fallah BN, Partridge MD, Olfert MR (2010) New economic geography and US metropolitan wage inequality. *Journal of Economic Geography* 11[5]: 865–895. CrossRef.

Fujita M, Krugman PR, Venables AJ (1999) *The spatial economy: Cities, regions and international trade*. The MIT Press, Cambridge, MA. CrossRef.

Gendron-Carrier N, Gonzalez-Navarro M, Polloni S, Turner MA (2017) Subways and urban air pollution. NBER working paper series, working paper 24183. CrossRef.

Glaeser EL, Gyourko J (2005) Urban decline and durable housing. *Journal of Political Economy* 113[2]: 345–375. CrossRef.

Greenstone M, Hornbeck R, Moretti E (2010) Identifying agglomeration spillovers: Evidence from winners and losers of large plant openings. *Journal of Political Economy* 118[3]: 536–598. CrossRef.

Harris CD (1954) The market as a factor in the localization of industry in the United States. *Annals of the association of American geographers* 44[4]: 315–348. CrossRef.

Harris JR, Todaro MP (1970) Migration, unemployment and development: A two-sector analysis. *The American Economic Review* 60[1]: 126–142

Head K, Mayer T (2004) The empirics of agglomeration and trade. In: Henderson J, Thisse JF (eds), *Handbook of Regional and Urban Economics*, Volume 4. North Holland, Amsterdam, 2609–2669

Head K, Mayer T (2006) Regional wage and employment responses to market potential in the EU. *Regional Science and Urban Economics* 36[5]: 573–594. CrossRef.

Henderson JV, Wang HG (2007) Urbanization and city growth: The role of institutions. *Regional Science and Urban Economics* 37[3]: 283–313. CrossRef.

Henderson V, Storeygard A, Weil D (2011) A bright idea for measuring economic growth. *The American Economic Review: Papers and Proceedings* 101[3]: 194–199. CrossRef.

Henderson V, Storeygard A, Weil D (2012) Measuring economic growth from outer spaces. *The American Economic Review* 102[2]: 994–1028. CrossRef.

Kofanov D, Mikhailova T (2015) Geographical concentration of Soviet industries: A comparative analysis. *Journal of the New Economic Association* 28[4]: 112–141

Kuzmenko L, Soldak M (2010) Monofunctional cities: Problems, support provision and development. *Економічний вісник Донбасу* 4: 83–88

Lall SV, Shalizi Z, Deichmann U (2004) Agglomeration economies and productivity in Indian industry. *Journal of Development Economics* 73[2]: 643–673. CrossRef.

Quintero L, Restrepo P (2017) City decline in an urbanizing world. Available from the authors upon request

Quintero L, Roberts M (2018) Explaining spatial variations in productivity: Evidence from Latin America and the Caribbean. The world bank. CrossRef.

Redding SJ, Sturm DM (2008) The costs of remoteness: Evidence from German division and reunification. *The American Economic Review* 98[5]: 1766–1797. CrossRef.

Roberts M, Stewart B, Prakash M, McWilliams K (2015) Global night time lights urban extents and growth patterns product. Alpha Version World Bank

The Heritage Foundation (2018) Index of economic freedom. Technical report

The World Bank (2018) Ease of doing business index. Technical report. CrossRef.

Vincenty T (1975) Direct and inverse solutions of geodesics on the ellipsoid with application of nested equations. *Survey review* 23[176]: 88–93. CrossRef.

Yoon C (2017) Estimating a dynamic spatial equilibrium model to evaluate the welfare implications of regional adjustment processes: The decline of the rust belt. *International Economic Review* 58[2]: 473–497. CrossRef.

## A    Concentration

Besides population decline, the region has presented concentration of population in fewer larger cities, which is precisely the prediction of Brezis, Krugman (1997) as a response to such a negative population shock. GINI coefficients for most ECA countries in table 5, for both population and night lights (NLs), support this. Only two countries show decreases in the population concentration, and the average growth in concentration is 0.51% per year overall.

Table A.1: Concentration of Population and Economic Activity

| | Population GINI | | | Change | | NLs GINI | | | Change | |
|---|---|---|---|---|---|---|---|---|---|---|
| | year 1 | year 2 | year 3 | | | year 1 | year2 | year 3 | | |
| Serbia | 0.507 | 0.507 | 0.7 | + | 1.81% | 0.564 | 0.558 | 0.785 | + | 1.87% |
| Kazakhstan | 0.508 | 0.542 | 0.651 | + | 1.34% | 0.64 | 0.725 | 0.739 | + | 0.74% |
| Russia | 0.608 | 0.629 | 0.758 | + | 1.17% | 0.756 | 0.795 | 0.834 | + | 0.49% |
| Bulgaria | | 0.628 | 0.68 | + | 0.83% | 0.768 | 0.776 | 0.782 | + | 0.09% |
| Belarus | | 0.668 | 0.713 | + | 0.67% | 0.831 | 0.837 | 0.804 | − | -0.15% |
| Albania | 0.696 | 0.718 | 0.756 | + | 0.41% | 0.77 | 0.783 | 0.814 | + | 0.27% |
| Poland | | 0.712 | 0.735 | + | 0.32% | 0.854 | 0.856 | 0.799 | − | -0.31% |
| Tajikistan | | 0.61 | 0.629 | + | 0.31% | 0.671 | 0.706 | 0.796 | + | 0.89% |
| Moldova | 0.656 | 0.708 | 0.688 | + | 0.23% | 0.775 | 0.768 | 0.787 | + | 0.07% |
| Kyrgyz Rep. | 0.644 | 0.676 | 0.671 | + | 0.20% | 0.799 | 0.797 | 0.811 | + | 0.07% |
| Romania | 0.622 | 0.63 | 0.641 | + | 0.15% | 0.679 | 0.695 | 0.685 | + | 0.04% |
| Ukraine | 0.737 | 0.735 | 0.744 | + | 0.05% | 0.834 | 0.891 | 0.814 | − | -0.11% |
| Uzbekistan | 0.674 | 0.652 | 0.65 | − | -0.17% | 0.826 | 0.817 | 0.82 | − | -0.03% |
| Georgia | 0.674 | 0.672 | 0.64 | − | -0.24% | 0.709 | 0.763 | 0.774 | + | 0.44% |

*Notes*: Estimated for the sample of cities which have both NLs and population data. Year 1, 2 and 3 refer to 1989, 1999, and 2010 (or the latest year available). In some countries one of these years might be different for one or two years. Table 1 shows specific years for the data available for each country. Change refers to the average annual change.

## B   Transition to Market Economies

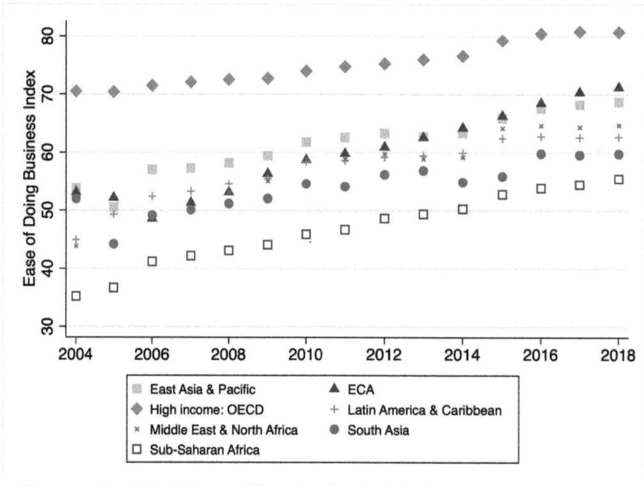



*Notes*: The Economic Freedom Index measures how economically free societies are, where freedom is understood as no government obstruction to the free movement of labor, capital, and goods (The Heritage Foundation 2018)

Figure B.1: Economics Freedom Index

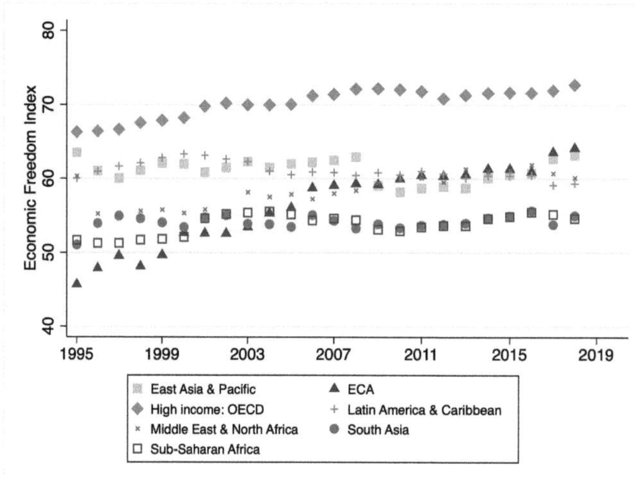



*Notes*: The Ease of Doing Business Index measures how fair and friendly economies are to medium and small private firms (The World Bank 2018)

Figure B.2: Ease of Doing Business Index

## C  Using NLs as a proxy of economic activity

Table C.1: NLs as proxy of economic activity

| Country | Log NLs | Constant | Observations | $R^2$ |
|---|---|---|---|---|
| Albania | 1.24** | -0.48 | 12 | 0.80 |
| Belarus | 1.25** | -6.43 | 6 | 0.84 |
| Bulgaria | 1.17*** | -6.04*** | 140 | 0.72 |
| Georgia | 0.88* | -1.19 | 7 | 0.6 |
| Germany | 0.72*** | 0.95*** | 1,980 | 0.41 |
| Kazakhstan* | 0.50** | 21.20*** | 28 | 0.13 |
| Kyrgyz Republic | 0.92*** | 0.21 | 7 | 0.66 |
| Poland | 0.61*** | 0.87*** | 325 | 0.94 |
| Romania | 1.07*** | -4.92*** | 210 | 0.67 |
| Russia | 0.33*** | 6.82*** | 456 | 0.98 |
| Serbia* | 1.26*** | -1.87 | 25 | 0.83 |
| Tajikistan* | 0.92*** | 13.17*** | 8 | 0.99 |
| Turkey | 1.40*** | 0.21 | 52 | 0.74 |
| UK | 0.56*** | 2.56*** | 840 | 0.28 |
| Ukraine* | 0.85*** | -0.69 | 135 | 0.5 |
| Uzbekistan | 1.01*** | 1.94 | 39 | 0.95 |

*Notes*: Column 2 shows the coefficient of a regression of log region GDP on log region aggregate NLs. Test is performed for for 16 of the 17 ECA countries analyzed (Moldova does not produce subnational GDP data). Robust standard error in parentheses. ***: $p < 0.01$, **: $p < 0.05$, *: $p < 0.1$. Countries with asterisks use raw nighttime lights; remaining countries used radiance calibrated nighttime lights.